D1635072

HOME

at Last

FREEDOM FROM
BOARDING SCHOOL PAIN

MARK STIBBE

malcolm down

PUBLISHING

Copyright © 2016 Mark Stibbe

21 20 19 18 17 16   7 6 5 4 3 2 1

First published 2016 by Malcolm Down Publishing Ltd.
www.malcolmdown.co.uk

The right of (author name) to be identified as the author of this work
has been asserted by him in accordance with the Copyright, Designs
and Patents Act 1988.

All rights reserved. No part of this publication may be reproduced,
stored in a retrieval system, or transmitted in any other form or by any
means, electronic, mechanical, photocopying, recording or otherwise,
without the prior permission of the publisher or a licence permitting
restricted copying. In the UK such licences are issued from the
Copyright Licensing Agency, Saffron House, 6–10 Kirby St, London,
EC1N 8TS.

British Library Cataloguing in Publication Data
A catalogue record for this book is available from the British Library.

ISBN 978-1-910786-41-3

Unless otherwise indicated, Scripture quotations taken from
The Holy Bible, New International Version (Anglicised edition)
Copyright ©1979, 1984, 2011 by Biblica (formerly International Bible
Society). Used by permission of Hodder & Stoughton Publishers, and
Hachette UK company. All rights reserved.

Scripture quotations marked (NLT) are taken from the Holy Bible,
New Living Translation, copyright © 1996, 2004, 2007 by Tyndale
House Foundation. Used by permission of Tyndale House Publishers,
Inc., Carol Stream, Illinois 60188. All rights reserved.

Scripture quotations marked (NKJV) taken from the New King James
Version®. Copyright © 1982 by Thomas Nelson. Used by permission.
All rights reserved.

Cover design by Esther Kotecha
Cover photo by Michael H/gettyimages.co.uk
Printed in the UK by Bell & Bain Ltd, Glasgow.

BSO

00021151

DEDICATION

To my dear, former housemaster, Geoff Hewitson, with love and gratitude for believing in me and exercising so much patience with the young man in the green shorts!

DATE DUE

			PRINTED IN U.S.A.

DISCLAIMER

I want to make it clear that for the majority of my ten years as a boarding school pupil I enjoyed a very privileged education with rich opportunities. The damage that was done to my soul occurred mainly – though not exclusively – in my first year at prep school (from the age of 8). So it wasn't all bad – far from it. I therefore want to thank the many staff and pupils of both my schools who were a positive influence on my life. I also want to thank my parents, Philip and Joy Stibbe, who did so much for me.

Having said that, my first year at prep school caused me a great deal of harm, as did several incidents during my public school years. I am not alone in having difficult stories to tell. There are many people who have written to me since learning about my work bringing a faith-based approach to boarding school pain, who have very deep scars. Where I have recorded testimonies here, I have in many cases changed the names of people involved in order to protect people's dignity and privacy.

CONTENTS

What Others Are Saying...   7

Foreword   9

Prologue   11

Introduction   15

PART 1: EXILE

1. A Christmas Carol   29

2. The Orphan Heart   41

3. A Painful Privilege   55

4. Shutting Down   81

5. Comfortably Numb   103

PART 2: HOMECOMING

6. Telling Your Story   121

7. Yesterday's Child   143

8. Restoring the Years   165

9. The Kintsugi Process   189

10. Angels with Beer   207

Notes   227

WHAT OTHERS ARE SAYING...

One of the biggest mistakes of my life was to choose to go to boarding school aged 11. From the moment I was put on the school train by my weeping father, I was sent to 'Coventry'! Months later, the staff relented but I had already boarded my heart. Many others have different yet equally devastating experiences. I am therefore so thankful to Mark for boldly and honestly breaking the taboo about speaking out about a system which was intended for good but actually took away many children's 'rights'.

In his book, Mark explodes the myth that being sent away from home will be 'the making of us' and invites us to dismantle the self-protective barriers that we unconsciously erected as children to deaden the pain of separation from home. Barriers that were accepted and even designed to make children into young adults way before their time. Barriers that enabled many to be more efficient and effective in institutional environments and other workplaces, whilst alienating them from their homes and families and the love they actually longed for but found themselves unable to give or receive. Mark understands this journey himself and describes the way we embrace compensating paths and patterns that ensnare us. He sensitively

assures us that it is never too late to change and shows us how we can take the necessary steps on our own journey towards a safe home coming in the arms of our Abba, Father in heaven.
Hugh and Ginny Cryer, founders of Culture Changers

In *Home at Last*, Mark has managed to address the abandonment many feel as a result of being sent away to boarding school and he has done so with honest vulnerability and spiritual insight. He highlights the wounds, walks us through the healing process and leaves us all with such a sense of hope. Hope not just to survive the hurts but to be healed from them by owning our stories, learning from them and walking taller because of them.

We believe this book has the power not only to heal, but also to bring full restoration, freedom and, above all, life!

It is well worth the read.

Tim and Sue Eldridge, Directors Presence Ministries International

FOREWORD

When a brilliant mind, a great storytelling ability, a life experience of brokenness and pain, and a man with the knowledge of a loving heavenly father who restores redeems and heals meet, you have Mark Stibbe. This book is the result of that convergence.

Although written about boarding school pain, as I read it my mind went to other groups who will be greatly helped by the truths contained within it. I thought of evacuees of WW2 like my mother or children of men serving long prison sentences, who will all be greatly helped. Others may just read it as a man's story, but they will be surprisingly moved, educated, inspired and probably healed in ways they never knew they needed.

Mark gives us a great insight into the purpose of this book: 'Many of you, like me, may have experienced and caused some pain as a result of the boarded heart. Whilst I believe we cannot change the way our story has progressed thus far, we can dictate the way it goes from here.'

Mark has given away a gift from his life journey and consequent healing, but it is a gift given away so that it can be passed on by you, the reader, so that others will in turn be healed and restored. Mark was once an author and speaker who I only knew by name, but he has now become my friend and I am proud to call him that and proud of what he is doing with his story, warts and all. Read, ponder and meet a man, his journey, his restoration and the God who will heal you also.

Paul Manwaring, Senior Leadership Team, Bethel Church, Redding, California and founder of Global Legacy

PROLOGUE

When I was a child, my father always used to utter the same refrain every time our car was within a few hundred yards of the house where we lived at the time. He would chant, 'Home at last, all dangers past.'

I'm not sure where Dad found this but he certainly loved it and he frequently uttered it. It always made me smile.

In the years leading up to my eighth birthday, the sentiments behind these words had considerable currency for me. Although my dad was a public school teacher, and we therefore moved a number of times, where we lived was always 'home'. There was no doubt about it. This was where I belonged. This was where I felt rooted. This was where I felt safe, happy too.

Then all that changed.

On 16 September 1968, I was sent away to prep school. From that day on, the value of the word 'home' decreased. The place I used to call my 'home' was now somewhere I visited. Nine months out of twelve, I lived in a country house in Berkshire, mingling with hundreds of other boys for whom 'home' had become a confused reality as well.

There was no mistake: home was now somewhere temporary. It was no longer a place of permanency.

For nearly fifty years, I lived with the legacy of this traumatic displacement. I remember when I was the vicar of St Andrew's Church, Chorleywood crossing the car park one day from the church to the vicarage. I was in my forties and I had been the incumbent for about five years by then. My predecessor, Bishop David Pytches, had long since moved on.

As I walked towards the front door, I thought, 'It's very good of David to let me be a guest for such a long time.'

In my mind, my house was not my home.

I was a visitor there.

Reading this, some may say, 'That's inevitable. Vicars are always moving in and out of houses that are not their own.'

The problem with this is that it applied to other houses too. After leaving Chorleywood, I bought a house in Watford. Now at last I would surely feel at home. Not at all – almost every day I would come downstairs in the morning, look at the long vertical window and the sun streaming through it, and think, 'How wonderful to be in a holiday house like this.'

In my heart, I was a temporary visitor not a permanent resident.

The ancient Greeks had two words that we can translate 'I live'. The first, *paroikeo* carries the connotation of a transient abode, such as a foreigner might feel passing through a place. The other word, *katoikeo*, also translates as 'I live' but here the connotation is of permanence. It means perpetually and continuously to make your home somewhere. Both words have *oikos* in them, which means 'house'. But *paroikeo* has the prefix para, which means 'adjacent to, nearby, not embedded in'.

For most of my life, I have been a *paroikos*.

I have felt like a stranger in every place I've called home.

Until now, that is.

In recent years, I have had to come to terms with the painful legacy of the ten years I spent at boarding school. I have been compelled, as a result of divorce and the loss of home and family, to face the things I didn't want to face about myself. In all of this, I have had to own the fact that most of my life I've felt like I've been visiting somewhere, passing through, not really belonging. Today I know where that feeling originated. I have experienced an extraordinary degree of healing. I have found a sense of 'home' again.

Home at Last is partly my story of how I developed a homesick soul, partly a collage of lessons I have learned about how we can find true recovery from the sense of exile that children feel when they are sent away from home for extended periods of time.

Put like that, this book may have much wider appeal than just the world of boarding school. One man who read some of an early draft remarked that he could relate deeply to what I had written. He hadn't been to boarding school but had been sent away from home during the Blitz in World War Two. This had given birth to a separation anxiety that had affected the rest of his life. The applications of my story are therefore more far-reaching than may at first appear. Although the subject may seem a bit 'niche', to quote one bookseller, its relevance is greater than we may imagine. Those whose childhood consisted of being sent from one foster home to another may relate to it deeply. Those sent away to live with relatives may find some comfort here as well.

Whoever you are, whatever your story, if you have a deep

longing to come home, then this is for you.

It's time to move from being a *paroikos* to a *katoikos*.

For all of us with homesick hearts, we're about to hear our Father sing, 'Home at last, all dangers past.'

INTRODUCTION

I realize now, looking back, that there rarely was a time while I was growing up when I was not in boarding school. At 8 years old I began ten years of boarding, first at a prep school and then, at 13, at a public school. There I spent nine months out of every twelve, coming home only at the half-term holidays. When I returned to my parents at Christmas, Easter and summer, I found myself within a boarding house again, this time at Bradfield College where my father was a housemaster. Even when we escaped as a family to the rustic seclusion of the Norfolk coast, the boarding world was never far away. Our house near Holt became the hub for many visitors – headmasters of Eton and elsewhere; former boarders, some of whom became our godparents; old friends of Dad and Mum, many of whom were teachers or alumni at boarding schools both near and far.

Before I started boarding school myself, I often used to wander down the staircase in the private side. Truly, in my father's house there were many, many rooms. In one half, there were fifty or so boys, all boarders, who slept each night in dormitories. In the other half, there were five of us in all – my father, mother, older brother, twin sister and me, who slept in our own rooms. In addition, there was our Labrador Bronte, our beagle Emma and our Siamese cat called Suzie Wong. My mother, completely ignorant that Suzie Wong was a celebrated Chinese prostitute, had given her this name. 'I liked the sound of it,' she said when one day she was challenged by my brother Giles. That cat would constantly pass from one part of the house to the other, somehow finding her way into the 'boys' side'. Maybe, conscious of her name, she went by night in search of men in need of comfort.

At the bottom of the staircase I would often stand and stare at the wooden door that stood between the private side and the strange, uncharted world where 'the boys' lived. I'd wander right up to that door and touch it, wondering if I was on the threshold to another world, like Narnia or Middle Earth. What was it like beyond that door? What kind of world lay on the other side? Who were these boys who strode in gowns, like marching crows, each day to the classrooms further down the hill?

One day, when all was quiet on the private side and the boys were home for holidays, I tried the door. It was unlocked! I slipped beyond onto a polished floor. I can smell it still today. Looking to my left, I saw a door half open. It was my father's study. There was a large mahogany desk beneath some windows. More books than I had ever seen were crammed into every space available on the shelves that ran like steps up several walls.

I tiptoed towards the desk and stared at the black and white photo of my mum – looking sideways, smiling like a film star. I smiled back. In front of it there lay a gilded knife for cutting open letters. I held it up to the light that streamed from the sunshine pouring through the windows. I thrust it forwards several times. 'The vorpal blade went snicker-snack,' I cried inside, quoting as my father had a thousand times the victory shout from *Jabberwocky*.

It was only when I put the worn blade down that I saw it. Lying in the corner of the study, behind the desk, there was a bamboo cane, leaning against the velvet curtain. It had bruised knuckles all the way down to its base and its wood was covered like an old man's back in light brown spots. Straightaway I knew this was my father's cane and that in this cosy place of leather chairs and books he must have wielded, when he had to, this whistling instrument.

At that moment, I understood that my father was not just kind and good but capable of imposing punishment. I would never stop adoring him, but something changed.

I did not only love him now.

I feared him just a little too.

And something more was shattered. No longer did I see the world beyond the door as magical. I saw it for what it was: a world where privilege and pain went hand in hand.

Within a year I would be deported there myself, not to the other side of my father's house, but to a prep school in the heart of Hampshire where I was beaten by a similar cane on four occasions in my first two weeks.

It was only half an hour away, but it seemed a million miles.

And it felt like exile.

THE BOARDED HEART

Today I write from the far side of catastrophe – a divorce and broken family, the loss of home, a decent income and a hard-earned reputation. All that left when I made decisions that in any moral scheme were wrong – choices that I've spent two years unravelling through formal psychotherapy and informal counselling. I know I chose the path I took and I cannot excuse my heartless actions as the reflex of a homesick soul. I have had to own my behaviour and its impact on others. This has led me on a journey to acknowledge that there were wounds from my past that formed in the fertile preconditions of my unfeeling choices. It took me nearly fifty years to see it, but now I see it clearly. Being sent away to school created what I have named a 'boarded heart'.

And I am not alone.

There are a growing number of psychologists who have realized that there are countless former boarders who have homesick souls and boarded hearts. Great Britain suffers from an untreated wound – a wound that affects the royal family, the criminal justice system, the police force, the armed forces, the institutional church, government, education, entertainment, the media, the secret service, business, and just about every sphere of society. Many in these different arenas betray this unhealed desolation. They succeed in what they do at work but they fail at what matters most at home. They masquerade in public as confident and smart while they are privately imploding. Many of these men and women are emotionally handicapped, incapable of empathy in their workplace roles and unable to enjoy liberty and intimacy with loved ones in their home and family. Many of them get married and then divorced, then married and again divorced. Many of them have children who grow up to repeat the same destructive cycle.

What is it that creates the potential for such distress? It is principally a British wound. We British were the first on the planet to endorse and cater for the abandonment of our children at the tender age of 7 or 8 years old. We were the first country to legitimize the exile of our young in institutions that its occupants compare to prison camps and cells. Oh yes, there may be other nations that have boarding schools, but I can guarantee these schools are found in countries that were once occupied by the British. They are a vestige of 'the British way of life' in which children learned to dull their feelings in the cold and lonely world of dormitories and desks. They are remnants of a system geared to forming men and women who could maintain a stiff upper lip in isolation and deprivation.

That may sound like an anti-imperialist rant but that is not my purpose. My purpose is to expose the emotional cost of the boarding school system. My purpose is to show you what you may not realize, that the primary spheres that dominate our culture – such as government, education, business, media, arts, and so on – are led by people who are hurting and we all know how the saying goes, 'Hurting people end up hurting people'. Our culture is by and large led by people who lost the capacity for feeling when they decided at a very young age that 'big boys and girls don't cry'. Our nation, in short, is led by what I call 'boarding school orphans'.

I know.

I was one myself.

FACING THE PAIN

At this point, some of you may be feeling angry because of what I've written. If you're a parent who has sent your children to boarding school, you may be protesting right now. 'What on earth are you trying to say? Our motives in sending our children away to school were good. We honestly believed it would provide them with the best education money can buy. We didn't turn them into orphans. We loved them.'

To you I respectfully reply, 'I don't doubt for a moment that your intentions were and are honourable. But it isn't your motivation I'm highlighting. It's the effect that being sent away to school may have had on the psychological, spiritual and social wellbeing of your child, both in the short and the long term. The focus is their hearts, not yours – on the consequences of their boarding school experience, not your reasons for sending them there.'

Then there may those of you who have jobs in the boarding school sector, say for example head teachers. Your complaint may be different. 'Are you trying to do away with the private schools? Is your talk of "boarding school orphans" some sort of socialist agenda for undermining the private educational choices available to parents today?'

My answer is, 'No! I am appreciative of all the positives of a private education. It's just that there are some very negative effects for children too. *If private schools could own and deal with these effects, it would be huge!* Imagine the nation being led by people who are no longer living with a homesick soul and a boarded heart! Imagine the impact of not only providing a cure but also a strategy of prevention within the schools themselves. So let me emphasize: I'm not trying to deconstruct the system. I want to see it transformed.'

Then there's a third reaction. This comes from those of you who may resent the fact that many have been able to enjoy a privileged education. If that's you, you may find it almost impossible to understand how people who have been away to such schools could in any way have suffered any kind of deprivation, even of a psychological kind. 'Who are you kidding? Boarding schools are for toffs. Toffs don't deserve any sympathy. They have everything.' To you I can only tell my story. I was sent away to boarding school on my eighth birthday. I watched my adoptive parents drive down a gravel road, leaving me standing by my trunk in front of a huge country house. That night I was beaten – six of the best with a cane. My only friend was my teddy bear, to whom I clung for dear life underneath the bed sheet. If that sounds comfortable, then all I can say is that it wasn't. It was hell and it has taken me nearly fifty years to get over it.

RESPECTING DIVERSITY

All this is not to say that every person who has been to boarding school ends up feeling or behaving like an orphan. In fact, there are often three types of ex-boarders I meet when I talk or write about boarding school pain.

Firstly, there are those who say, 'I loved boarding school. I have met with old boys since and we have always reminisced about "the happiest days of our lives".' One woman described it as 'one huge sleepover'.

Then there are those who say, 'I tolerated boarding school. My home life was extremely toxic, so going away to boarding school was a welcome relief. Although I suffered deprivations, it was the lesser of two evils.'

Finally, there are those who say, 'I hated boarding school. It felt like a terrifying abandonment and the deprivations I suffered

– especially separation from parents and home – have negatively impacted my entire life.'

While the lines between these three responses can be permeable for some, they are broadly speaking representative. If your experience was universally positive, then I am truly thankful.

For many others this has not been the case. There are more than we could ever count who were permanently scarred and who have never had an opportunity to speak about it to anyone. Indeed, they may have vowed in their hearts to keep silent about it. Many who have been damaged by boarding school find it almost impossible to talk about it because they have come to believe that to do so would be to commit the unpardonable sin – ingratitude. Maybe they even had to recite these lines from *King Lear* at school: 'How sharper than a serpent's tooth it is to have a thankless child.'

Maybe those words were ingrained upon their soul.

I know they were on mine.

If so, it's time to break this collective silence and it's time for the healing to begin.

THE HOMESICK SOUL

For effective healing and liberation to happen, I am convinced that more than a psychological approach is needed. I respect the work being done by other champions in this field but, in my view, they lack one important, indeed vital ingredient – a spiritual approach. Yes the insights of human psychology and psychiatry can prove immensely helpful but if ex-boarders are by and large boarding school orphans then my experience tells me this: children separated from their mums and dads carry father and mother wounds and these are only ultimately healed by the intervention and infusion of a spiritual reality, and this I call 'the Father's love'.

What do I mean by 'the Father's love'?

Boarding school girls and boys have daily been compelled to say the Lord's Prayer. If my experience is anything to go by, this enforced repetition rendered the words fairly meaningless for most pupils and at worst distorted the image of God as an approachable and ever-present Father. But there is a life-changing disclosure at the very beginning of the prayer, unrecognized by most schoolchildren: 'Our Father, who art in heaven'. Jesus called the God who fashioned the universe, 'Our Father'. In the language that Jesus spoke, the word is *Abba*. This translates as something like 'Dad' or 'Papa'. And that one word is life-changing for boarders and ex-boarders.

Most boarders and ex-boarders are blighted by what I call the 'homesick soul'. In their hearts they cry, 'Where are you, Dad? Where are you, Mum?'

For many years, I have written many books and spoken at many conferences in many countries on this subject. This is what I have discovered. *There is not a place on this planet where the orphan heart is not found and where the Father's love is not needed.*

My approach is therefore unashamedly faith-based, specifically Christian-based. It is based on the view, borne out by my own story, that only the perfect love of our Heavenly Father – a love that can also come to us also in a mother-like way – can fill the hole in the soul and free us from our exile.

Only the Love of all loves can heal the homesick heart.

Only the fire of the Father's love can open up the boarded heart.

This is not the religion of the private school chapel, where

God is so often distant and remote. This is what Jesus had in mind for us – an intimate relationship with his Dad and ours. It is something we can all experience, not the reserve of the few. It is an invitation to everyone, however much they have failed and fallen. It is the gift that the Father wants to give to all those who have experienced desertion of whatever kind, including the desertion by their parents at boarding school.

SPIRITUAL HEALING

This is why I have written this book. While I respect the two other books presently on this subject – *The Making of Them* and *Boarding School Syndrome*[1] – both in my view lack a spiritual dimension to the healing process.

For example, both books fail to provide a diagnosis of the impact of boarding school life on the *soul*. If worth and belonging are fundamental needs in every human being, then what are the consequences when they are removed through the boarding school experience? Is the healing of such shame and homesickness a purely psycho-therapeutic process or is there a vital spiritual component these approaches miss? If men and women suffer from orphan hearts, does it not stand to reason that they need to find healing in the arms of the true and perfect Father? As King David sang in Psalm 27, 'Even if my father and mother abandon me, the LORD will hold me close' (Ps. 27:10, NLT).

My conviction is this: we need to have a spiritual understanding of the trauma of being sent away to boarding school, and we need a spiritual dimension to the healing of that trauma.

That is why I have chosen to write a book in two parts. In Part 1 we look at what I call the 'cycle of pain'. The boarding school wound is one involving four deep impacts to the soul: desertion, deprivation, disengagement and dependency. Only when we see the spiritual implications and consequences of these four components will we properly and thoroughly diagnose the wound that afflicts so many.

In Part 2 we look at the 'cycle of healing'. Here we embrace the four stages of the healing journey: revelation, restoration, reconnection and recovery. These exactly correspond to desertion, deprivation, disengagement and dependency. These four stages of the healing journey are all, in one way or another, spiritual in nature. They are four stages in the soul's homecoming. They are four steps towards the Father's house. They must be experienced if we are to enjoy the long-awaited end to our spiritual winter.

In all of this, I will tell some of my own story.

In telling my story, I want to encourage those of you who are boarders or ex-boarders to come out and tell your story too. Share with someone you trust. When we tell our stories, our shame is no longer a secret and when our shame is no longer a secret, it loses its capacity to control our lives.

And have faith too!

Many of you, like me, may have experienced and caused some pain as a result of the boarded heart. Whilst I believe we cannot change the way our story has progressed this far, we can dictate the way it goes from here. With our Father's help, we can move our lives along a new trajectory – a redemptive arc in which we no longer live with homesick souls but healthy hearts, and where we no longer live with shut-down hearts but learn to work with emotional intelligence.

So take heart.

Be brave.

And let's start this epic journey together, trusting that by its end we will all have found our freedom – a freedom that will bless beyond all words the people that we treasure most.

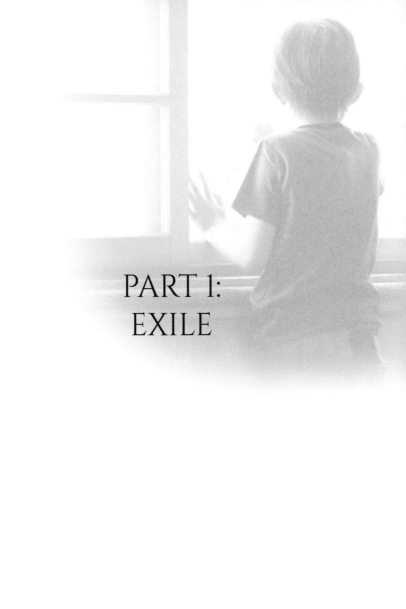

PART 1:
EXILE

1. A CHRISTMAS CAROL

When I was studying English at university, I found it hard at times to forgive Charles Dickens. His novels are gargantuan. Each one would take a ten-week term to read, let alone digest, but I was given groups of two or three to study in a fortnight. Why oh why did he have to write such lengthy and laborious tomes?

Then I discovered *A Christmas Carol*. I had seen the film – the best adaptation for grown-ups, starring Alistair Simms – when I was a boy. My father and mother had taken me, along with my brother and my twin sister to a cinema in Norwich to see it. I was mesmerized, haunted even – especially by the third and final ghost.

Then, as a student, I eventually got round to reading it as part of my course. What a relief it was! Here was a novella, not a novel; a book that could be read in under a day not a month!

And what a cracking story Dickens tells.

Ebenezer Scrooge, the most miserly of men, stingy beyond description, frozen and aloof, controlling and dictatorial, makes everyone's life a misery. He is as cold as the snow outside.

He refuses to give to those raising money for the poor and he resents the pleas of his employees for time off to spend with their families at Christmas. He is truly the most despicable of men.

But then on Christmas Eve Scrooge is startled from his sleep by the ghost of his former business partner, Jacob Marley.

Marley is in perpetual chains.

Marley declares that Scrooge is about to be visited by three ghosts whose purpose is to warn him to mend his ways before it is too late and he too finds himself a restless spirit bound by clanging manacles.

Scrooge is momentarily startled but then falls back asleep.

Sure enough, the ghosts come.

The first phantom shows Scrooge some scenes from his past life, highlighting in particular moments of great sadness designed to reveal what Scrooge has repressed through the hardening of his heart. The second shows Scrooge how the people with whom he interacts each day truly view him. The third presents a chilling picture of where Scrooge is heading – to a lonely death, an unattended funeral, a parlous legacy, an eternal nothingness.

As Scrooge is shown his old grey gravestone, a panic rises in his soul. The clock is ticking and his time is running out. He yearns and pleads for just one last chance to put things right.

And then the dawn breaks.

Scrooge awakens from his fitful sleep and celebrates that he is still alive. He resolves to make amends, rejoicing at the second chance to redeem himself and live a life of generosity. He gives freely to the poor and, most of all, gives all he has – indeed his very heart – to help the disabled son of his longsuffering employee. Tiny Tim is the boy's name, and at the end of the story the child gives his audience a much-loved benediction: 'God bless us, every one!'

SOLITARY AND NEGLECTED

I'm sure that many of us are familiar with this story, both the original script and the many (nearly fifty) cinematic versions. But do we really know it? Do we truly appreciate what Dickens is trying to convey here? In particular, do we realize how Dickens drops some clues into the story to try and help us understand why Scrooge became the man he did?

The most important hint comes early on, when the Ghost of Christmas Past takes Scrooge back in time to his prep school. It is clear from what Scrooge's sister says that their father has for years been very hard on him, leaving him at school when the other boys had left for home and Christmas holidays. This is what the ghost reveals:

> 'The school is not quite deserted,' said the Ghost. 'A solitary child, neglected by his friends, is left there still.'
> Scrooge said he knew it. And he sobbed.

In remarkably and indeed unusually few words, Dickens refrains from telling us why Scrooge became the cold, unfeeling miser that he was. He simply shows an incident from his past – an episode in which a single word begins to form in the careful reader's soul.

Abandonment . . .

Scrooge was abandoned. He was left alone, left behind, at boarding school. The school may not have been deserted, but Scrooge was. The agony this caused is described in two simple adjectives:

Solitary . . .

Neglected . . .

Scrooge is the only one who has not gone home for Christmas. He has been forgotten. Separated from his family and his home, his misery is compounded. Not only was he abandoned at the beginning, when he was sent to school, but now he is abandoned again, left in exile all alone when he should be at home, around the fire, enjoying fun and food.

No wonder Scrooge hates Christmas. Every Yuletide is a grim reminder of this moment when he felt the stabbing pain of separation. Every Christmas is a re-enactment of the greatest sadness in his life – the crushing loneliness of abandonment.

How the Wheel Turns

I may have been a little hard on Dickens, lamenting the length of his stories, because he was in fact a genius. No one has ever understood the orphan plight more clearly and more insightfully than him.[2] Many of his stories have orphans as heroes, most memorably *Oliver Twist*. But how many of us have ever seen Scrooge in this light? How many of us have understood that Ebenezer is an orphan too?

Dickens' appreciation of what I call the 'orphan heart condition' is something yet to be fully celebrated by the literary critics. He saw with astonishing clarity that a person like Scrooge was a boarding school orphan, and this is the wound in the core of his soul, the trauma that informs his personality and his destiny, the hurt that shapes his later habits.

What do we learn, then, from Ebenezer Scrooge? We learn that there is a cycle of pain, one that has the power to rob a person of their very soul.

At the start and the heart of this cycle, there is the experience of abandonment. The child sent away to boarding school feels deserted. They feel the aching pain of separation from parental love. It is this sense of being 'deserted' (a word that Dickens actually uses in the previous quotation) that lies at the heart of Scrooge's life. It is the thing that brings him to tears.

'And he sobbed.'

That three-word sentence says it all.

Here Dickens is effectively issuing a warning to the reader. He knows full well that Scrooge will be remembered for his stinginess, aloofness and unfeeling cynicism. But this is not all there is to Scrooge. Dickens wants us to see the root behind the fruit. He leaves clues within the story so that we can see the pain that lies behind the personality.

It all begins with desertion. Scrooge is effectively turned into an orphan. Separated from a father's love, he is completely alone. It then proceeds to deprivation, as Scrooge is robbed of all the blessings that children experience at home.

It then progresses to detachment, as Scrooge shuts down emotionally, disengaging as a means of protecting his heart and surviving his ordeal.

It ends with dependency, as Scrooge becomes obsessed with money, controlling others through his work and finances

See how Scrooge is determined to keep his heart from ever dealing with the sense of shame engendered by becoming a boarding school orphan.

This is how the wheel turned for Scrooge.

It is how the wheel turns for those who feel the pain of being orphaned by their parents when they're left behind at school.

THE CYCLE OF PAIN

As much as I want to distance myself from Ebenezer Scrooge, I find it very hard. There is more of Scrooge in me, and more of me in Scrooge, than I would ever want to confess.

I too have been round this cycle.

First of all, I experienced desertion. However much my parents didn't want this to be so, the fact is I felt abandoned when I was left behind on the gravel drive in front of the red-bricked porch at my prep school. I can still see the car, that had carried me and my brand new trunk, departing from the grounds and heading for the home I loved. I will never forget that feeling. My parents had told me that this was going to be a great adventure and a priceless privilege. They had a dream, a noble dream, to give me opportunities that others could never touch or taste. But all that made no impact at that moment on my racing heart. My hands were trembling. My eyes were glancing round at my surroundings, longing to lock on to some familiar face or landmark. But finding none, I simply stood and stared, wondering when I'd see my parents, brother, sister, dogs and cat again. Like Scrooge, I felt alone and deserted. I wanted to cry, but somehow – through some Herculean effort – I managed to keep the tears at bay.

And then I experienced deprivation.

This is a paradox, I know. I was in a country house with magnificent grounds, in a location that would cheer the hearts of countless *Downton Abbey* fans. But I felt robbed of the things that I had seen as part and parcel of my normal life. Where was my parents' love? Where were my beloved brother and twin sister? Where was my dog? Where was my home? Where was my bedroom? The 'new normal' was deprivation. I was just going to have to get used to it.

So I chose detachment.

Fearful of being told that I was 'wet', I decided to shut down. I removed my emotion chip, to use the language of the character Data in *Star Trek: The Next Generation*.[3] I vowed within my soul that I would never feel again. Feelings were for 'sissies'. To survive the next ten years my feelings would have to be frozen. I would have to become a mini adult at the age of 8 and 'grow up' early. This was the only way I knew to survive the trauma of abandonment. I would simply have to go through life emotionally disengaged, unhooking myself from others to avoid the risk of emotional attachment.

This in turn led to dependency.

No one can completely eradicate the aching pain of homesickness by simply choosing not to feel. I found comfort through activities and substances. At prep school, football was my great obsession. I found a buzz, a rush, a thrill in sporting excellence that compensated for the loss of significance, security and self-worth. At public school, I found the same through sex and drugs and rock and roll. I tried to fill the gaping void with food and alcohol as well, even academic work.

Do you see how the wheel turns?

It isn't just in Scrooge's life.

It's in the life of every orphaned boarder.

It isn't just fiction.

It's fact.

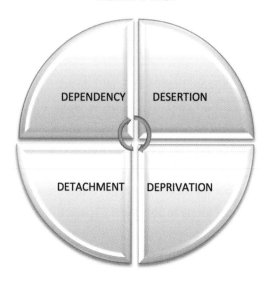

A LONG-TERM LEGACY

For Scrooge, of course, the long-term consequences of this loss of parental love, this exile from his home, were huge. Perhaps one of the most significant moments in *A Christmas Carol* is when the Ghost of Christmas Past takes Scrooge back to the time when he left the girl he fell in love with when he was a boy. In former times, Scrooge and she were paupers and so they loved without condition, but now Scrooge is a young man and something else has stolen into his heart. She calls it 'gain', meaning the accumulation of money. Scrooge denies it, but his manner gives his heart away. He is indeed in love with money now and she, having none, is a woman without means. The outcome is inevitable. The young woman confronts the man she loves. Even though they made a contract many years before, with tearful eyes the heartbroken woman releases Scrooge. Her last words to him are heartbreaking:

'A very, very brief time, and you will dismiss the recollection of it gladly, as an unprofitable dream, from which it happened well that you awoke. May you be happy in the life you have chosen!'

She left him, and they parted.

'Spirit!' said Scrooge, 'show me no more! Conduct me home. Why do you delight to torture me?'[4]

In these few but resonant words, we see the long-term legacy of Scrooge's abandonment. He is simply afraid. As his beloved says before her parting words, 'You fear the world too much.' Terrified of being abandoned once again, Scrooge seizes control and abandons his beloved so that he will never be the victim of her possible abandonment of him.

Here we see the fruit from the root. The root is abandonment. The fruit is coldness in relationships, a growing disengagement from those who might have cause one day to betray him, a stout refusal to express feelings and a closing of the door to intimacy. With Scrooge, we see the consequences of the trauma of boarding school pain – an inability to trust the world enough to love and to be loved; a frozen heart, a shut-down soul, a distancing from intimacy.

No wonder Scrooge breaks off his long engagement.

No wonder he is so incapable of feeling for the little children in his adult world who suffer so, especially Tiny Tim.

Scrooge is lost indeed.

THE FRUIT AND THE ROOT

And so are we who suffer like him. Those who have researched the boarding school wound have found a catalogue of toxic consequences in former boarders. In her book *Boarding School Syndrome*, Joy Schaverien lists the bad fruit in the lives of many a male ex-boarder. Many turn into

- A high achiever with no language for emotions
- An intelligent person with little emotional intelligence
- A loving person who dare not love
- A masculine-identified man with early homosexual experiences[5]

Often this internal turbulence is suppressed until a man enters mid-life, when the wound begins to take its toll on relationships. As Joy says, 'The resulting psychological conflict may be masked until the middle years of life, when the armoured – and often socially successful – personality may break down. This is when the distressed child within the adult may emerge and overwhelm the defensive structures that have until then served so well.'[6]

With female ex-boarders the loss of loving care from their parents, especially when going through puberty, may cause lifelong damage. Joy Schaverein talks about the culture of the female boarding house – a culture where sexuality is repressed and where girls are taught to subjugate their needs to those of others. The results of such an ethos are obvious in later life: female ex-boarders often lack the freedom to articulate emotions and enjoy true intimacy. As one such sufferer reports, 'I have learned to live a life without knowing how to love anything or anybody properly.'

THE LOSS OF EMPATHY
I am not alone, and nor is Dr Schaverein, in spotting the long-

term consequences of the boarder's pain. Recently my wife and I went to see our favourite comedian perform a virtuoso performance of stand-up entertainment. Bill Bailey is his name. I'm sure you've heard of him – a modern-day reprisal of the ancient court jester, as hilarious as he is hairy.

Bill spent two and a half hours brightening up our lives with musical routines performed on a bewildering range of, often exotic, instruments. He also told stories and recited poems, made observations and engaged in rants that had us rolling in the aisles. It was an unparalleled cocktail of musical talent and comic creativity.

In the course of one of his reflections, Bill engaged in an extended critique of the political parties and their leaders in the UK. Suddenly, while describing the current cabinet, Bill used a phrase that identified in a nutshell why our country is being governed by what Nick Duffell calls 'wounded leaders'.[7] He described the team on the top table of government as 'Eton-scarred'. There was no barb or malice in the comment. Yet it took my breath away.

My belief is that many institutions in our country are led by men and women who have been scarred by boarding school and who wear what Joy Schaverein calls 'armoured personalities'.[8]

The evidence is everywhere.

A few months back, I was invited to a dinner in a London club. A few of us from our old boarding house were invited to meet our much-loved and now retired housemaster.

At the bar after the meal, I stood with two men who were exact contemporaries of mine at school. As the conversation and the whiskey flowed, it transpired that I was going through a divorce while my two friends, both prominent in the legal profession, were going through a second and a third respectively. Nothing could disguise the pain. Our failure to remain in loving marriages was the outward evidence of our inner turbulence. The wounded child within all three of us was starting to emerge, clamouring through fractured lives and broken homes for resolution.

The only difference between them and me was that I was halfway through receiving two-years of psychotherapy, during which I had begun to see the damage caused by boarding school and, through the help of a brilliant counsellor, had started the process of healing. Thus it was that even though I was in the middle of the break-up of my marriage, one of them – a judge – said, 'Mark, it's good to see you looking so content.'

That was a 'light bulb moment' for me. For the first time in my life, I was beginning to feel the deep serenity that comes when the boarded heart is opened and the healing starts.

My homesick soul was coming home.

My fractured self was being made whole.

There was still a long way to go – maybe there still is – but the possibility for finding freedom was emerging, a freedom that now I'm called to give away to those who still remain imprisoned in their pain.

2. THE ORPHAN HEART

On my eighth birthday, my life changed forever. Until that day, I had learned to trust the world again. Having been given up for adoption at seven months, along with my twin sister Claire, this had been a challenge. By the time I reached my seventh year, however, I had truly started to feel secure and happy, carefree even. My adoptive parents were kind, loving and generous. My sister and I and our brother enjoyed great holidays and constant treats. Indeed, I remember taking a flight to Edinburgh with my mother when I was 7 years old. It was my first time on a passenger plane and the experience of accelerating down the runway was exhilarating.

'Do you know what?' I said to my mum when we were at 35,000 feet.

'What darling?'

'This is the best year of my life.'

'That's a lovely thing to say.'

As we sped to Edinburgh to stay with my Scottish godmother, all seemed well with the world. Seven is the perfect number. This was my perfect year.

But then the skies began to darken.

I was told that I was to be sent to boarding school on the 16

September. This was 1968. Our grandfather had left money in a trust for us to have the best education money could buy.

'The world will be your oyster,' my parents said.

I didn't question this, although I didn't understand why oysters were involved.

In my mind, I had learned to trust again. My sister and I had been abandoned by our birth mother. That kind of thing would never happen to us again. We were safe now, enjoying the golden age of our childhood.

Or at least that was what I believed.

LEFT BEHIND

As the first school day drew closer, my heart became more anxious and the questioning began.

'What if I am homesick?'

'What if I have no friends?'

My mother, noticing my apprehension, took my favourite teddy bear called Edward and hand-knitted exactly the same uniform that I would be wearing: green cap, blue shirt, grey jumper, grey shorts, and so on. The night before I left for boarding school, she came into my bedroom and gave me what she called 'a butterfly kiss'. This was our nocturnal ritual. She would nibble my ears and I would giggle. She would too.

'Here,' she said passing me my bear.

'He's in my new school uniform!' I cried.

We laughed before she left my room. After she had gone, it was hours before I finally succumbed to sleep.

The next day all my school belongings were neatly packed into a black trunk. Dad and Mum carried it to the car and Edward

Bear and I got in the back after I'd said a tearful goodbye to my sister and my dog.

The drive from home to school was not that long, maybe half an hour, but I remember wishing it would last forever.

We took a sudden turning and there it was – a country house standing tall before a gravel drive.

'Here we are,' Dad said.

I grabbed my teddy tight. My heart was racing now.

'Come on Polo,' Dad exhorted. Polo was his nickname for me – short for Marco Polo, a name that simply came from Mark, which turned to Marco, and then Polo snuck in behind when none of us was looking.

I climbed out of the car and walked towards the porch, my new black polished shoes crunching on the stones. A suited man with silver hair and jet black, bushy eyebrows strode out onto the gravel. His smile revealed a set of bright white teeth. His inky eyes were shifty and unsettling.

'Feel free to leave,' he urged my parents. 'Your son is safe with us.'

But safe was far from what I felt. I held fast to my mum as she leaned down to kiss my head – a rather formal gesture born from years of bowing low before the god of middle-class respectability. And then the car doors shut.

The engine started.

I started to wave goodbye, holding up my teddy's paw.

I saw my mother's hand sneak through the quarter open window, her golden wedding ring glinting in the warm September sun. I have never felt as lonely as I did right then, as our family car manoeuvred past another convoy of arriving, teary sons and left the grounds to take the road back home.

TROUSERS DOWN

The first night at my boarding school, I dropped a bag of marbles on the wooden floor. I was on the third storey of the house, outside the door to my dormitory. The plastic bag split open and the multi-coloured spheres went crashing down the wooden stairs, right down until they clattered into oak and stone outside the door that ominously said, 'Headmaster'.

Up he came, snorting like an angry bull.

'Which one of you boys did that?' he shouted, wielding a gnarly cane like a cavalry sword.

'Me, sir,' I trembled.

'Right, trousers down.'

And so the beatings started, the first of four within my first two weeks; six of the best on my bare backside in view of other new boys who had wide-eyed stares and gawping mouths; six strikes with a knuckled cane, causing thin red stripes and livid bruises on my tender skin.

I couldn't stop the tears as I lay and shuddered on the bed, once the tyrant and his instrument of torture left.

No one said a word.

I clung fast to Edward Bear.

'Lights out,' a matron called an hour later, after checking we had all been through the washrooms, performed our nightly ablutions and were now tucked up in bed.

Then, with the flick of a switch, darkness fell.

That night, as other boys whispered to each other, I cowered underneath the sheets, clasping Edward to my chest.

All I wanted was my mother.

I missed her gentle nibbling of my ears.

I missed her prayers, her fond goodnight and her calming liturgies. 'Sleep tight. Mind the bed bugs don't bite!'

I missed my father's strong and reassuring form appearing at the door, checking all was well.

I missed my dog and I missed my bed.

That was the first of many nights when I looked forward to my sleep. Sleep became the only place where fear could, by and large, not threaten me. Sleep was my escape – a country where my bear and I could flee from waking terrors like the cane; a landscape where I could reunite with those I wouldn't see or hear for months on end; sleep became the haven for my homesick soul.

And so it all began. I would fall asleep and then awake at the sound of matron shaking an old bell around our ears. Then, like POWs, we would stumble from our beds and shuffle over freezing floors to lavatories and basins, gearing up to start another day of discipline.

MIND AND HEART

How does a young boy or girl react to such events?

In my case, I experienced a division in my soul between what I thought and how I felt. At the level of thinking, I reasoned that my parents had to be right and that these years away at school would give me great advantages in life. I therefore repeated in my mind the same old mantras I had heard in the countdown to my first day at school.

'You'll enjoy the best years of your life.'

'You'll have the finest education money can buy.'

'You'll be set up for life.'

'You'll be able to go to Oxford or Cambridge.'

'You'll have the world at your feet.'

In essence, all of these statements amounted to the same thing: 'This will be the making of you.'

However, at the level of emotion, a voice told me the exact opposite: 'This could very well be the breaking of you.' The reason for that was simple: I felt abandoned, alone and afraid.

Such ambivalence is very common. Countless ex-boarders testify to the same division of thought and feeling – reasoning in their heads that their parents knew best but feeling in their hearts a crushing sense of loneliness and exile. This separation of thinking and feeling began for them and me on the very first day at school. For many it is never resolved.

SPIRIT, SOUL AND BODY

What we are talking about here is a severe wounding – the fracturing of the soul. To understand the nature of this fracturing, we need not only to understand how the human soul is constituted but also how we are created or designed as a whole. When you see the word 'design' in matters to do with the universe and human beings, it's not long before you see the word 'God'. Here I make no apology for introducing theistic and indeed Christian language into the discussion. According to a Christian worldview, human beings are made in the image of God. God is three persons but one single being or substance. The three persons of the Godhead are the Father, the Son and the Holy Spirit. These three persons co-exist in an eternal interdependence of love. At the same time, they are one God even though they amount to three persons.

This 'three-in-one' or 'triune' nature of God is replicated in human beings, which stands to reason if we are created in God's likeness. Human beings are tripartite beings. They are made of spirit, soul and body. What then is the difference between these three?

The word 'spirit' (*pneuma* in the Greek New Testament), is the part of us which is designed to commune with God. Separated from God, our spirits are dead. Reunited to God, they come alive. They are quickened and born anew through being connected to the source of life itself. From a Christian perspective, such an awakening comes through the experience of conversion – through renouncing a life of self-rule and allowing Jesus to reign over one's entire life instead.

Then there is the soul (*psyche* in Greek, from which we get the word 'psychology'). Whereas the spirit is designed to relate to God, the soul is designed to relate to ourselves. The soul comprises our mind, heart and will. This is the part of us that thinks, feels, reasons, imagines, chooses and so on. It is the intellectual, emotional and volitional aspect of our nature.

Then there is the body (*soma* in Greek). If the spirit relates to God and the soul relates to itself, the body communes with the external world of the senses – to other people and to our environment.

SPLIT SOUL SYNDROME

God's desire is that we should experience peace at all levels. The word peace has a holistic significance. Right from the beginning, our loving, Heavenly Father wanted us to enjoy wholeness and harmony in our relationship with him, our relationship with others, our relationship with our environment and our relationship with ourselves. We could say that this wholeness has three different applications: up (with God), out (with others and with our world) and in (with ourselves).

When a human being experiences a great wounding, our peace or wholeness is radically disrupted. When we experience a severe trauma, everything in fact is knocked out of kilter. In particular, the soul becomes fractured. The thinking part of the soul may seek to give a rational explanation and justification of the wound that we have received, or indeed that we have inflicted. The heart on the other hand is not so interested in such a cognitive response. The heart feels something devastating – guilt, shame, abandonment, rejection, sadness, grief, anger, rage, betrayal, and so on.

When I was left alone at my prep school on my eighth birthday, my soul split in two. Part of me thought that this had to be for the best because I trusted my parents when they told me it would be the making of me. At the same time, another part of me felt completely the opposite: that this was going to be more a breaking than a making. I felt abandoned. I felt left behind and left alone. I felt deserted by my father and my mother even though I knew in my head that this was not their intention at all and that they would be horrified if they knew for a second that I felt that way about them.

NAMING THE WOUND

The problem in my case is that this was not the first time this had happened to me. When my twin sister and I were born, we were left in the hands of some nuns and placed in an orphanage in north London. Our biological father had left the scene and didn't even know his former girlfriend was pregnant. Our birth mother, unable to cope, had entered a home for unmarried mothers in Hackney, with the intention of giving us up for adoption. Seven months later, she left the home and returned alone to the Midlands. My sister and I were adopted by Philip and Joy Stibbe. Philip was by then a teacher at a public school in Berkshire.

There are two things I want to say about this part of my story. The first is that this separation from my birth mother initiated a splitting of my soul. On the one hand, I understood from Joy Stibbe, my adoptive mother, that my birth mother had wanted the best for Claire and me, that her act of giving us away was motivated by a deep desire for us to have a better life than ever she could give us on her own. In my heart, however, I felt abandoned. I felt like an orphan, which of course is what I was.

This splitting of the soul began to happen when I learned from early on that my sister and I were adopted, or 'adocted' as our older brother called it. Part of me thought our birth mother had noble intentions, wanting us to have a better life. Another part felt forsaken.

When I was left at prep school on my eighth birthday, exactly the same fracturing occurred. I responded intellectually by saying that my parents were justified in doing this. I reacted emotionally by feeling abandoned, deserted and forsaken. History, in other words, repeated itself.

The second thing I want to say is that the two experiences of being orphaned and being sent away to boarding school are very similar. When force of circumstances dictated that I simply had to receive extended psychotherapy at 52 years old, I came to see that I had owned the first experience (being abandoned by my birth mother) but had not dealt with the second (being abandoned by my adoptive parents). Clearly, the thinking side of me had won in the battle between my head and heart. I had intellectualized my pain, justifying the second trauma with the mantras I have mentioned. What I hadn't ever faced was that this second wound, the trauma of being sent away alone to boarding school, was just as devastating as the first. As I faced this trauma with my psychotherapist, I began to describe it as 'my second orphaning'.

This, then, is the heart of it. When little children are sent away to boarding school, they are orphaned in all but name. Their parents may be still alive but to all intents and purposes, they are far away and will remain so throughout childhood. The conclusion is inevitable: this experience turns boarders into orphans and boarding houses into orphanages.

THE ORPHAN HEART

I have written extensively on the orphan heart condition in books like *I Am your Father* and *My Father's Tears*.[9] What I have never done is apply these insights in a systematic way to the experience of being sent away to boarding school.

So what do I mean by the orphan heart?

The orphan heart is created by a perfect storm involving the combination of a negative event and a negative emotion.

The negative event is separation. In my case, this happened twice. I experienced separation from my biological parents as a baby. I then experienced separation from my adoptive parents when I started boarding school. In both cases, the event was traumatic. It caused a negative emotion in my soul.

By that, I mean shame.

Here we need to be careful in our use of language. Very often we confuse shame with guilt but they are two entirely different realities. Guilt is a 'doing' word. Shame is a 'being' word. Guilt is born out of what I do. Shame is much more about who I am. Guilt is therefore like a verb; it is engendered by what we do. Shame is like a noun; it is more of a state of being, engendered by what has been done *to* us, or by what has not been done *for* us.

Perhaps the best way of describing shame is by saying that it is a feeling of being unlovable, unloved and unlovely. It is the feeling of being defective in some way. As others have argued, guilt says, 'I've *made* a mistake.' Shame says, 'I *am* a mistake.'

How then does shame relate to separation? When a child is separated from parental love, they inevitably begin to believe a lie. That lie goes something like this: 'If I had been a better child, if I had been more lovable and valuable, then I would never have been sent away.'

That is the voice of shame.

Shame is the feeling of being unworthy of love and belonging. It is a negative belief caused by a negative experience – in this case separation from the love of a father and a mother. Shame is utterly toxic, leading to the poisoning and paralysis of the soul.

When a child is separated from their parents' love, shame begins to cast its shadow on the soul. The result is the birth of the orphan heart condition, a perfect storm in which separation combines with shame to create the shipwreck of the soul.

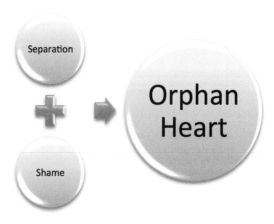

JOANNA'S STORY

Shame can be especially destructive when a child comes to believe that they were sent away to school because they were too naughty at home, or simply not good enough as a child.

A friend of mine called Joanna, wrote this:

> When I was 8, I was enrolled at a small boarding school for girls located in a large, imposing stately home in the Derbyshire Dales. Before I went, my mum told the headmistress that she would have problems with me. 'Joanna can't be good for very long,' she said.
>
> I don't remember whether this was ever mentioned to me directly, or within my hearing, but my guess would be that I was very aware of the problem that I had become – probably overly aware. I remember being an extremely sensitive child, to the point that the smallest of things would impact me deeply. Just as a 'butterfly child' is sensitive to light and touch, so I would blister and burn at the very hint of perceived criticism or failure.
>
> My mum's memory (thirty years after it happened) is of my form

teacher ringing to say that they had been left with a 'monster' and asking what my mum planned to do about it. My mum's response was that the headmistress had assured her that they would be able to cope with me and therefore it was up to the headmistress to deal with it. I think by then my mum had reached the end of her capacity to know how to help me, though she had earnestly tried. It wasn't that I was a rebellious child; in fact, I wanted to be good so badly. When I was good, I was very good. But it never seemed to last. Always I would mess up again, with uncontrolled outbursts that seemed to turn me into an agonizing problem for others.

By my teenage years, I was being sent to doctors and child psychologists but nobody had an answer for what was 'wrong'. Electrodes were stuck to my head to see if I had epilepsy but nothing explained my immense struggles to manage with life.

With no answer to give them, I ended up with a deep belief that I must be inherently bad and unacceptable. I had no 'deep dark secret' to explain my emotional struggles, nothing to explain to other people why I couldn't cope with life as other children could.

This testimony is a striking example of exactly what I mean by the orphan heart condition. When a child experiences separation by being sent away to school, a feeling of shame begins to cast its shadow across the soul. The negative experience of being abandoned leads to negative beliefs about the self: 'I am not good enough to deserve to grow up at home.' 'There must be something fundamentally wrong with me.'

No More Secrecy
All this reveals why dealing with the pain of being sent away

to boarding school is so important. While it is true that not everyone's experience is negative, it is also true that many were permanently damaged by their abandonment and have believed ever since that they were and are defective, fundamentally flawed, not worthy of love and home.

This is why I have started retreats and webinar courses on the healing of boarding school pain. This is why I have written this book to accompany these courses and retreats. It's time to start speaking to each other about our orphan hearts. It is time to let the wounded inner child articulate its pain. It's time to start sharing our stories. As author and speaker Brené Brown has said, 'Shame hates it when we reach out and tell our story. It hates having words wrapped around it – it can't survive being shared. Shame loves secrecy. When we bury our story, the shame metastasizes.'[10]

It took a lot for Scrooge to face the consequences of the separation from his father and his mother's love.

It will take a lot for us to do that too.

But Scrooge's story heartens us along the way, inspiring us to recognize that we are not alone as we confront our orphan hearts.

The Holy Ghost, our comforter, will lead us from the orphanage and guide us to the Father's house, where arms and hearts and doors are open for us, waiting for the homesick souls to travel home at last.

3. A PAINFUL PRIVILEGE

In 2013, an ex-boarder called Josy published an open letter to her boarding school. In it she addressed her old school as a former lover. She imagined she was dancing with him. During the letter, she began to explore her deep ambivalence towards her boarding school experience, describing first the things she loved and missed:

> We swayed and I thought about only the good things. Your scent crashed over me like a wave of familiarity, like coming home. I wanted to inhale you: your peanut-butter-toast, shrimp stir-fry, coffee with a trace of dish soap. Your late-night popcorn, butter that lingered in the air for hours.

But then, after only these brief sentences, a different note began to emerge:

> I hated you for your empty playgrounds. I hated you for your scheduling disasters and course conflicts and your general sense of apathy. I hated your library hours. I hated your cold showers and your cinderblock walls and your endless mass of cloud. Mostly, I hated you for giving me beautiful people and then taking them away.

I hated you for your history; for the way your desks pulsated with one thousand fingerprints. As if every wall had been leaned upon before, every doorknob clutched. It was like being your 234th wife. Some silly agreement I didn't even remember consenting to.

We swayed and I thought about all the times I almost broke up with you. All the times I wanted to scream and cry and say that what you do is wrong. But is it? You weren't actually unfaithful. You simply outlived your marriages. Just as I knew you would outlive ours.

Tomorrow, you would cauterize our relationship with a Senior ring, a rose, and a diploma. And that would be the end of it. I played out the scene in my head like a movie. I imagined it would be one of those slow, dramatic departures: me, in the backseat of a rental car, with my rose and my ring, resisting the urge to turn and look for you through the window. Me, with my ring and my brimming tears, wondering if you were watching me go. And hoping you were.

But we both knew that tomorrow you would not be watching me at all. And I hated you for that. I hated you for moving on.

Tomorrow, you would be preparing for a new crowd: guileless teenagers and parents and mountains of cardboard boxes. Kids ready to fill drawers that you promised to keep empty for them. Drawers that meant: things were about to get serious. And after some weeks of unpacking, some arguments about who was supposed to take out the trash and who was supposed to shovel the snow, these eager children would learn exactly what it means to lie in bed with you.[11]

FROM DESERTION TO DEPRIVATION

Those who have never been through boarding school may have little understanding of the oxymoron I want to explore in this chapter – painful privilege. For many it is impossible to conceive how spending ten years in such an apparently comfortable and idyllic environment could be anything other than an enviable luxury, afforded only by the rich, enjoyed only by the few. Unless they have been a close relative of an ex-boarder, or had to work with one, they may have little idea how countless young men and women have paid a heavy price for going through this system, especially in their feelings and friendships, their souls and their sexuality. Yes, it was a privilege, but it was immensely painful to many as well.

As we look at the cycle of pain again, what we're exploring here is the second part headed **deprivation**.

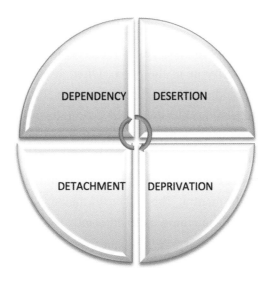

In the last chapter we looked at desertion and saw how the cycle starts with a child being told that they are being sent to boarding school, usually with a legitimizing mantra: 'This is the best education money can buy. This will set you up for life. It will be the making of you.' This is often uttered with some kind of emotive qualifier, such as, 'Your father and I have saved up so you can have these opportunities. We have sacrificed a great deal. Your grandfather put the money for your education in a trust and at great personal cost,' etc. All this acts as a rational justification, but it doesn't in any way help the child when they are left on their own at the entrance to a large building – often an old country house – with nothing but a trunk and sometimes a teddy (if the school allows them). The child may know in their head that they are about to enjoy a great privilege, but in their heart they will more often than not feel the acute pain of being left alone, far from home.

The emotion the child may now feel is one of abandonment. The car, driven by the parents, leaves them with their worldly goods on the drive or in the porch. Often, a younger sibling, come to say goodbye, leaves with the parents. The exiled child is left behind feeling a loneliness that may, unhealed, plague the soul for the rest of his or her life.

This trauma of separation then leads to an inevitable split in the child's soul between thinking and feeling. In their mind, the child repeats the mantra: 'This will be the making of you.' In their hearts, they feel something quite different. 'This is unbearable; it will not make me. It will break me.' At this point, the child effectively becomes a boarding school orphan.

As a result of the loss of attachment to parents, the boarder may now start to believe the lie that they have been left because they are not good enough to stay at home. Toxic shame begins to attach itself to the wound of separation. It breathes its vile deceptions into the boarder's heart. 'It's because you're a problem that you've been sent away.'

At some point shame then morphs into fear. The child starts to feel afraid of their new surroundings, their peers, the bigger boys or girls, their teachers and other staff. Everyone else seems larger, stronger and wiser. They appear confident, self-assured, well-adjusted and arrogant.

Once the child feels this sense of being deserted and abandoned, they become aware of the level of pain involved in the privilege. In other words, they become acutely aware of the paradoxical fact that this place of apparent abundance is also the landscape of deprivation. They become aware that they have been robbed of things that are of crucial importance, relating to the most fundamental needs in the human soul.

Once this reality hits them, children start to feel a gnawing and visceral ache in the pit of their stomach.

This is the homesick soul.

Some never recover from it.

Overcoming Your Guilt

'How can you say a child who experiences this level of privilege is deprived? Their education is elitist and exclusive. How dare you make it sound as if you and they were denied basic human rights? Who do you think you are?'

I wonder if you've ever heard this kind of reaction to the idea that boarding school is a painful privilege, an experience of deprivation within a context of plenty. Anyone who is courageous enough to speak out on this subject, such as Nick Duffell in the 1990s, is almost certain to meet this kind of hostility, which is perhaps one of a number of reasons why so many have kept silent for so long. It isn't just the sense of being ungrateful that persuades a person to become silent about their sense of exile from the ones they loved. It is guilt too. The ex-boarder may well grow up feeling that they have no right to lament their boarding years, when so many of the people they work and live with have had far fewer opportunities in their education. Guilt gags their mouths, and in the process amalgamates with shame into a potent drug that creates a kind of permanent paralysis of speech.

If the ex-boarder is to find freedom and healing, then they must get over their commitment to secrecy and silence. They must not only own up to their feelings of desertion, if indeed they had them. They must also admit to the deprivations they experienced too.

What kinds of deprivation, then, are we talking about?

For the rest of this chapter I will list just some of the deprivations experienced by the boarder. This is not exhaustive. Nor are all of the items experienced by every boarder. However, these are the main laments that I have frequently heard during over thirty years of listening to people talk about their pain. Some I have uttered myself.

Here are the seven most common statements of deprivation from ex-boarders. We will look at each of them in turn:

'I was deprived of love'
'I was deprived of home'
'I was deprived of safety'
'I was deprived of childhood'
'I was deprived of siblings'

'I was deprived of innocence'

'I was deprived of freedom'

We will explore each of these briefly.

'I was deprived of love'

When I was left at my prep school on my eighth birthday, it became very quickly evident that while some of the teachers at the school were kind, and some of the other boys too, they were not and could never be a substitute for the love that my father and my mother had given me.

This is one of the heartbreaking realities about the boarding school system. When a child is left at the doors of some great country house or mansion, effectively for three quarters of every year for the next decade, they are separated from both their parents' love. When I was left behind, the only form of communication I had until half-term was handwritten letters. These I treasured. Many I still have in my possession today. There were no mobile phones on which you could send a text for help and then receive some reassuring words from home. Nor were there computers on which to write a hurried, furtive email. I just had to own the fact that I was now separated from parental love, at least until those weeks when the family car would trundle up the gravel drive again and take me home.

What everyone concerned must understand is this: to all intents and purposes, a person who is separated from their parents' love becomes an orphan. What is an orphan but a person who has been deserted by their parents? This desertion may come as a result of death, disease or, as in this scenario, distance. But an orphan they are. They are deprived of a basic human right – a child's experience of parental presence, parental love.

Many seek to compensate for this loss of parental love through developing a particular affection for an older male teacher or a matron. These become for them a kind of surrogate father, mother too. But neither can fill the father and mother-shaped void in the abandoned child's heart. They may compensate in part, but they can never be a total, effective substitute for the parental love the child has lost.

Piers Partridge, a psychiatrist and a former prep school boarder, made this remark on the 1994 BBC documentary, *The Making of Them*:[12]

> Perhaps the most fundamental issue about boarding is that no matter how well meaning the boarding schools are, no matter how committed the staff are, they do not give the children in their care love. So when you put a child in boarding school you are talking about putting a child in an environment without love for maybe three quarters of the year at an age at which love is so important to that child.

Instead of a father or a mother, the institution becomes the parent and the institution, as Josy's letter at the start of this chapter reveals, cannot love you! Sometimes a child is actually told that the school will become a substitute for a parent. John Wormald, who also appeared on the TV documentary, provided this poignant recollection:

> My mother said that one of the reasons that she sent me away to prep school to board was that it would be a substitute for my father

who had left us and wasn't there. The problem with that of course was that the school wasn't and couldn't have been an adequate substitute for parenting by a father, and of course I lost my mother into the bargain as well.

There is no getting away from it. Boarding school children are deprived of love.

'I was deprived of home'

There are probably few people in the United Kingdom who have a greater appreciation of what 'home' means than the boarding school pupil. Only those who are habitually exiled from their homes as children can truly understand what the ache for home entails, what the ecstasy of homecoming feels like deep within the human soul.

I well remember being driven from our home the half an hour to my prep school on my very first day. I longed for Dad to turn around and drive me home. When I was being dropped at the entrance of the school, I longed for my parents to have a change of heart and take me back. That first night, my buttocks bruised and my eyes red, I hid beneath the sheet and blanket on my bed and longed to fall asleep and then awake at home, in my own bed, relieved that I had woken from some ghastly dream.

I longed constantly for home; for waking up to the familiar sound of rooks and pigeons in the trees outside my bedroom windows; for trundling aimlessly downstairs to receive a royal welcome from our dogs; for mum standing by the Aga getting breakfast ready; for sauntering down to a football pitch and pretending to be my soccer heroes with my friends; for spending long hours on the floor of my bedroom, recreating battles with my Airfix soldiers; for evenings watching *Dr Who* with my brother and my sister.

It felt like all of that was gone and I was now some prisoner of war, destined to spend years and years as one unimportant soul within the ranks of boys – at desks by day, in dormitories by night.

For some, of course, the boarding school is the far, far better place. When home becomes a battlefield – a place much scarier than school – then none of this is quite so relevant. The word 'home' loses its currency. It crashes on the stock market of the child's soul and becomes a worthless commodity. School becomes the safer place – a place of order and predictability, not chaos and dysfunction. I know that this is true. For several years while I was in my teens, my home was just like this, and so my school became the place where I felt safe and happy too.

But for many this is not so. Home is where their hearts are. Home is what they yearn for. As one 11-year-old prep school boarder called Alexander said in the TV documentary:

> I really do like it here. It's a really nice place, really good food, really good grounds, friends . . . but at home I guess it feels like you're near your toys, near your pets, you've got your mother and you've got your father and your family around you. And then here you've got . . . well, about all you've got from home that you can really cuddle or anything is your teddies, but you don't need them much.

Later Alexander described how he felt as he saw the school for the first time and his parents' car drove away:

I remember seeing the bars on the windows that night and thinking, 'Oh, flip.' I really, really, really didn't like it. The second I saw the wheels go past the gate and the back of the car . . . I felt like I was just being dumped here. And . . . I thought, *three weeks* . . . One of the older boys found me crying behind one of the lockers. Most people don't like it that much when they come here but they get used to it.

They get used to it.

What Alexander meant, if I may be presumptuous, is that boys and girls learn to survive. Whether they ever get used to the homesickness in their soul is another issue. Many go through life longing for home and never really finding it. Many go from the institution of the boarding school into professions in other institutions, such as the Bar, the Church or the army. They do this because they have come to see the institution as their home.

I know.

I was one of them.

It is here, then, that one of the most glaring differences lies between boarding schools and day schools. The day school pupil gets to go back home each afternoon, to dads and mums and to their own beds at night. The boarder has no such luxury. They only see their mums and dads infrequently and have to live in strange beds for a decade of their childhood.

'I was deprived of safety'

If home is a place of security for a child, then being sent away to boarding school can represent a sudden, stark transition. Having only known the protective covering of a parent's love, they now find themselves under the oversight of unfamiliar men and women, not all of whom are safe.

I remember as if it was yesterday the feelings I experienced on my first day at prep school. While my parents were still standing with me on the drive, the headmaster was a model of manners, wit and charm. A child's instincts are, however, tuned to other frequencies than simple courtesies. I sensed that all was not quite right and that the man with silver hair and jet black bushy eyebrows on my right was dangerous. Call it intuition. Call it a nascent gift of discernment. Whatever it was, I knew that what this man presented to my parents was a mask, and that once they'd left a different face would break from underneath the smiling one he showed.

And that is precisely what occurred.

As soon as Dad and Mum departed, his tone was gruff and harsh.

'Go inside and don't run.'

That night he beat me.

In the next two weeks, he beat me three more times.

Fortunately, that cruel man only lasted until the end of my first year and was replaced by one of the kindest men I ever met during ten years of boarding – a grey-haired, avuncular man, who looked and acted as if he'd just walked out of the pages of *Goodbye Mr Chips*.[13] When the governors put him in charge, the reign of terror was terminated overnight. The years that followed were happy ones for me. I was never beaten again.

For others, their experience was far more traumatic. Just a month or so ago I mentioned that I was writing about boarding school pain during a talk I gave at a church. Afterwards an elderly man, at least in his late seventies and more likely in his eighties, came to me in tears.

'Thank you, thank you, thank you,' he cried.

When he had recovered enough to speak, he explained.

'I was sent to boarding school when I was a child and abused terribly – beaten routinely and violently for years.'

He paused between his sobs.

'I have never recovered from it.'

I offered a steadying hand.

'I vowed,' he said, 'that I would never send my boys away to school and when the time came, I kept my promise.'

This is the reality for so many boys and girls who have gone through the boarding school system. Yes, things have changed for the better in this area, but men and women who are now advanced in years still live with haunting memories of past abuse in their boarding schools. Many, being deprived of safety in their childhood, have been deprived of life itself, living in the half-light of their shame, somehow navigating through the shadows and surviving as best they can, just as they had at school.

When I put a notice up on Facebook last year, sharing that I was thinking of devoting part of my life to the healing of boarding school pain, the responses were startling. One man wrote this:

The worst part of boarding school for me was from age 11–12 because of the beatings. It was a miracle if we did not get a beating every day. You got caned for each Maths question you got wrong. Any spelling mistake was a cane each. Class 'mean' scores were 90 per cent. Anyone who got less received a cane for each mark less. It was not unusual to get up to 50 beatings in a day. We had light bleeding on our backs and scars that lasted for years. The school was the best in the nation at the time and produced top students, so parents felt it was worth it.

For many children boarding school was not a safe experience, even if it is safer now. Even now, however, a child may well feel deprived of safety the moment they start boarding. The beatings may have disappeared but other threats still lurk within the ancient walls and spacious halls. There is the shadow of abuse and the threat of bullying which are much tougher to monitor than they are in day schools. When you have between 40 and 50 boarders being overseen by only a handful of staff, it is all too easy for dangerous people to operate unnoticed. As Nick Duffell points out:

> There is little protection. Anyone who has tried parenting knows how difficult it is: imagine one housemaster and a matron trying to take care of a house with 40 boarders. Even with recent social advances, such as Britain's Children's Act, no level of vigilance is going to work with such numbers.[14]

It is no exaggeration, therefore, to say that many boarders can feel deprived not just of love and home but safety too.

'I was deprived of childhood'

Looking back, I realize now that at some point during my first few weeks at boarding school I tripped a switch within my soul. I recognized that in order to survive this experience I would need to grow up really fast. Put another way, I chose to become a mini adult at the age of 8. This effectively deprived me of the ten years of my childhood from the age of 8 to 18. Yes, I did many of the things that children of those ages do. But inside my heart, I had become a small version of an adult, a grown-up well ahead of time. Today I realize I was robbed – deprived of much of what could have been a normal childhood. While it's true that I gained a lot, it's also true that I lost a lot. I can now see how, in the following thirty years or more of my life, I sought so desperately to rediscover it. In other words, I unconsciously reversed the process. Having been turned into an adult when I was still a child, I then spent years trying to be a child when I was in fact an adult.

Benedict Cumberbatch is arguably one of the greatest British actors of this present generation. His reinterpretation of Sherlock Holmes has, in particular, won him many awards and accolades. He is an acting genius. His recent starring role in Hamlet was immense. The tickets for his performance sold immediately. The response was unprecedented.

At the same time, Benedict is an ex-boarder and someone whose experience was, in his own words, 'just crap'. No wonder, then, he has written so powerfully about the rights of children. No wonder he has spoken out against those who rob children of their childhood. Having been through this experience, he has a passion to see this prevented.

One recent Christmas, Benedict wrote a letter to Father Christmas:

Dear Father Christmas,
So my friend has asked me to write to you . . . I have to confess it's been hard to know what to say. Mainly because like most adults I

feel preposterous asking anything of you because our time with you is surely done. Now we get our own presents, control our own fates, take responsibility for our own actions, and live in the world we have created . . . so it's not for us to turn around and plead for your help with the environment, the migrant crisis, the NHS, education, food banks, human rights, fundamentalism and wars. Though God knows we need all the help we can get with all these man-made problems and more.

And it's not that you aren't compassionate and full of joy. You're great. In spite of you being changed into different colours for corporations and being bastardised to represent materialism gone mad – despite probably originating in some season based pagan druid ritual a million thought miles from requests for spontaneously combusting hoverboards . . . Kidadults cynically pointing this out after having their moment of belief in you are wasting everyone's precious time. Because you are not for them. You are for the children. Children who need some magic in a world where the borders between innocence and responsibility, playful imagination and cold, adult obstacles are continually shrinking.

This is what I'd like to ask you to help with. A little more time for children to be children. Stretch the moment of magic and playfulness. Distract them from the realities of a world gone mad so that they can laugh with their breath rather than sob with their tears. Especially those caring for family members, or suffering illness, hunger or poverty. Especially those hiding in buildings as bombs rain down, or being handed shaking with fear or cold into a boat to escape environmental disaster or war. Please help to light up their worlds with a moment of joy and hope.

When I think about it you've got it tough this year . . . And when

I really think about it I'm not sure that asking you for a lightsaber and getting one (not that I ever did by the way) is equitable with controlling the space time continuum and making the good of childhood last a little longer.[15]

Only someone who has themselves been deprived of their childhood could have written that.

'I was deprived of siblings'

I missed my twin sister when I went away to school. We were adopted as babies and so have a very special bond to this day. We shared a pram when we were very little. We often shared a bedroom when we went on holiday, regaling each other with stories after fond goodnights with Mum and Dad, whispering our outlandish tales across the space between the beds. No wonder we are both full-time writers and storytellers today. Those years until the age of 8 were golden ones in which we played together – chiefs and squaws, doctors and nurses, giggling like there was no tomorrow. Yes we had our moments, but by and large my memory is of two imaginations united constantly in flight and soaring well above the clouds of ordinary life.

My older brother was a special influence upon my life as well. To be honest, I did not always see a lot of him. He had an enormous Hornby train set in the attic of the house and spent a lot of time up there sending his trains around a landscape he had fashioned. But he was the best of brothers and remains that way today – loyal to the core and kinder than any other man I've met, besides our father, whom he resembles more than anyone.

Going to my prep school brought an abrupt and unwelcome

end to this closeness to my siblings.

Until, that is, my brother's life imploded.

Giles had been sent to another prep school not far away from mine and was deeply homesick. Dad and Mum decided that they would have to move him from that school to mine. My school decided that they wanted me to be my brother's mentor for his first few weeks, steering him through the unfamiliar ways of his new school. That was strange for us both. My brother is two and a half years older than me. The norm in my school was for boys about two and a half years older to look after the younger ones, not vice versa! However, this strangeness quickly wore off. I became my brother's protector for a fortnight or so, guiding him through those daunting days and helping him to settle in. Since that time, we have always looked out for each other and been there for each other in a crisis.

This unusual episode at my prep school was brought back to remembrance when our father died. At his memorial service in Norwich Cathedral, our uncle Paul – his younger brother – stood and delivered a brief tribute. This is a paraphrase of one of the things he recollected:

When I was sent away to prep school, my older brother Phil had been there for several years. He knew that I would miss home and need some gentle reassurance, so he devised a plan. We discovered that our dormitories were on the top floor of two buildings that stood parallel to each other, separated by a quad. Just before lights out each night, Phil would stand on a chair and look across the way from the window of his dormitory. I would do the same. He would wave to me and I would wave to him. Those waves are what got me through those difficult days. They have got me through more than a few since. I will miss them.

It is hard for those who go to day school, and who therefore return to their siblings every afternoon, to comprehend the wrench that I'm describing here. Of course there will be some who say, 'My siblings were such a nightmare I would have loved to have been sent as far away from them as possible.' Others may respond, 'This was not my experience. My siblings and I ended up in the same school and saw each other a lot.' For others, however, the loss was deep and permanent. Here is Joanna's story:

My brother Stephen is a year older than me. When I was 7 he went away to a small boarding school for boys in the Yorkshire Dales. There is a photo of him in his school uniform standing on our lawn at home. When my mum and I looked at it a couple of years ago, while sorting old albums, she noted that it must have been taken on his first day. How did she know? Because apparently his beloved teddy, Sleepy, who was happily peaking out of the overnight bag on his shoulder, only made it for the first three weeks at school. On the first leave-out, Sleepy came home and was apparently cast aside. Bullying in boy's schools back then was rife and I don't want to even imagine the cause of Sleepy's excommunication (or the wound it created).

Though not aware of details, I am very aware that Stephen had it much harder than I did at my boarding school. I have a feeling that corporal punishment was still in practice, and certainly, when he moved to public school, at around 13 years of age, there were things going on there that no boy should ever have to endure.

Sadly, my brother has gone through years of severe mental health problems (what my parents believe to be bipolar depression) and seems to have decided long ago to have nothing to do with me.

I have never known him as an adult. I was very unwell as a child, with severe difficulties coping in life, and perhaps it is easier now for him to cut me off completely.

Has he forgiven me for where my difficulties robbed him of the childhood he could otherwise have had? I don't know. Maybe the pain of the past is too deep. Letters and cards written to him, sent to the boarding schools where he has recently lived and taught, have never been answered. I do not even know if they have been read. It breaks my heart, but I know God has promised to restore the years the locusts have eaten.

I am told there was a time, in the very early years of childhood, when we loved to play together and I truly seemed to adore my big brother.

One day I believe we will be together again, able to open up our hearts and reconnect in the way God originally intended.

For those who went away to school, the loss of relationship with their siblings may not have been temporary. As in Joanna's case, the damage and the deprivation may have lasted for decades.

'I was deprived of innocence'

For the child who doesn't board but goes to day school, their questions about sex, and indeed their first sexual experiences, are overseen – at least in part – by mums and dads. Not so in the case of boarders. For many, their first sexual experiences may well occur within the boarding school itself: often, but not always, with the same sex if it's a single-sex boarding house; sometimes, though not always, through an abuse of power by older pupils or by staff. While this is not unknown within non-boarding schools as well, the boarder does not have the overarching canopy of parental love. Their parents simply are not there in the way they are for those who come back home at 4 p.m. and whose weekends are not spent in some secluded country house but in their living rooms and at their family meal tables. For boarders, sexual innocence can be lost in situations where no one can offer explanations or support, unless of course the truth comes out.

Let me tell you the story of a close friend.

His first sexual experience occurred during his prep school years. He was about 10 years old at the time and a matron in her late teens or possibly her early twenties took a liking to him. Some nights she would come secretly and collect him from his dormitory, taking him up a flight of stairs into her rooms. There she did things to him that he did not fully understand. His heart, separated from his mother's love, yearned desperately for the next nearest equivalent to that embrace. The matron, standing in for mothers, not just for him but scores of boys in the school, seemed to him to meet that need. In the absence of any sex talk from his dad, he fell right into her arms and would have kept on doing so had the matter not been exposed a few months later in the most unusual and extraordinary of ways.

He went to stay with his grandmother – his dad's mother. He loved staying with this amazing woman whom his family knew as 'Granny Leicester'. She played table tennis right into her advanced old age and made stew and dumplings that were delicious. She had a Yorkshire terrier called Joey and a chauffeur called Mason. My friend idolized her, so he was looking forward to this time away during the holidays.

However, for reasons that he can't recall, she put both his dad and him in the same room, side by side in separate beds. At some point during those two nights, my friend started to sleep talk. Evidently he was dreaming of the junior matron, calling out her name and speaking in a way that betrayed at once his loss of innocence.

Next morning the father sat down beside him on the bed.

'Son, I need to talk to you.'

He shuffled for a moment.

'You can tell me anything. You know that, don't you?'

'Yes.'

'And you know I won't be cross.'

'Yes.'

'Last night you were sleep talking, in a way that told me someone's touched you where they shouldn't.'

My friend was the one shuffling now.

'Is there anything you should tell me?'

And out it came, the whole story. The father was extremely kind and reassuring, as he always was, but he phoned the headmaster and that was the end of the matron's time at the prep school.

Over forty years later, my friend shared this with his psychotherapist. It took a lot to do that, but when he had, she looked at him and said, 'You've counselled people for decades, haven't you?'

'Yes.'

'What would you call that experience?'

My friend paused and then spoke softly, 'I'd call it sexual abuse.'

The loss of sexual innocence at boarding school follows many diverse narratives. My friend's story arc is not the only one. But for many, the journey from ignorance to knowledge, from innocence to experience, was and is traversed by lonely boys and girls, far from home, separated from the normalizing preparation and interpretation of a loving dad or mum – unless of course they sleep talk in their holidays.

For some boarders, their parents simply aren't the kind in any case that would have helped. Their homes were dysfunctional, their parents absent or argumentative, their opportunities for being listened to at best occasional. As one woman shared with me, 'Sexual abuse and corrosive verbal messages around body image and capacity to achieve was rife – so destructive on so many levels . . . but the process of going away, albeit abusive, was a sanctuary from home, and going home provoked anxiety. There was some excitement returning to school. However, going to school felt like not being protected and I had to survive independently.'

There is so much more I could say here, especially about the messages about sexual love communicated to the soul within the artificial world of boarding houses, but I'll leave the last word to Nick Duffell:

There are many problems with being institutionalized from puberty. We tend to think that adolescent children do not need their parents much; but this is a fallacy. They need loving homes to come back to at the end of a day where they can be safe, regress if they need to, talk things through or remain silent, as they wish.

When they begin their forays into the exciting but difficult world of courtship, children get support by living in a home with parents, who after all made them through an act of love. In single gender institutions they do not learn about the opposite sex, and they leave with unrealistic expectations. The hot-house atmosphere of sexual excitement – the prime condition of puberty, which is generally neither understood nor properly supported by their school staff – can cause terrible stress for those who are on the receiving end of others' fantasies. So co-ed boarding is no solution . . . At puberty, a child deprived of loving touch may sometimes become a magnet for those who are also lonely, or for paedophiles who may win their trust with a friendly word, with catastrophic outcomes.[16]

'I was deprived of freedom'

I was brought up by a father who had been a prisoner of war. For nearly three years, he slept in dreadful conditions, on simple mats beneath flimsy bamboo shelters, side by side with ranks of starving, beaten men. If he was alive today, there's something I would ask him: 'Dad, did boarding school prepare you for these hardships? Did being sent away to school enable you to face these deprivations of your freedom?'

I'm convinced he would have said yes.

It is no coincidence that countless boarders old and new have likened their experiences of boarding school to prison. This is often said in jest but then there's never a truer word . . .

Boarding school prepares a woman and a man for loss of liberty. Ex-boarders who have been imprisoned, either through being sinned against, or sinning, have switched into the surviving mode they learned at school.

There are, of course, great costs to this obsession with timetabling. Boys and girls whose lives are regimented by the clock and bell are often robbed of times in which they do not have to do but simply be. In the competitive, performance-driven world of the boarding school, simply resting and thinking, being and imagining, is something for those precious moments between going to bed and falling asleep. The motto is 'I do, therefore I am'. It is not, 'I am, therefore I do.' As Nick Duffell has reflected,

> In boarding school every moment is organised, regimented and marked on a timetable. Whether it be work, games, or routines to do with the body, the programme is set. No time for hanging around, riding around on bikes, moping around, loafing around, messing around – vital for teenagers! In consequence, one symptom frequently reported by ex-boarders and their spouses is over-work, overinvestment in the *doing* side of life, at the expense of *being*.[17]

Deprivation and Detachment

In these seven ways, and no doubt many others, boarders have to face head-on the oxymoron of their privileged pain. They are, we are, deprived in a place of plenty, which is in some ways the most absurd and punishing of paradoxes.

What happens when a child faces such basic deprivations?

The answer is simple.

They dull that part of their souls where empathy is born and intimacy forged.

They move into survivor mode.

They grow up faster than they should.

They become mini adults overnight.

They lose up to ten years of their childhood.

They shut down.

They become grown up on the outside, while remaining wounded children on the inside.

They develop what Joy Schaverien calls 'the armoured self'.[18]

They cultivate a boarded heart.

4. SHUTTING DOWN

I don't know when it was exactly, but there was a moment when I found myself beneath the covers of my bed, holding back the tears. The lights were out and the other boys were quiet. I was clinging tight to Edward Bear, wincing from the bloody bruises on my flesh after yet another arbitrary beating from the sadistic, silver-haired headmaster. My 8-year-old heart was trying to process what was happening to me as I reeled from the shock.

Why am I here?

What have I done to deserve this?

Where are my parents?

When I am ever going to go back home?

Then the lights went on. Not in the dormitory but in my soul. *No one's coming to get me. I'm stuck here, along with Edward Bear – just the two of us. Somehow, someway, I'm going to have to get through this. No one's going to help me. I'm going to have to do it on my own.*

With that realization, something else began to shift. The tears dried up. My feelings froze. I turned my emotion chip off. From that time on, I would not hug my Mum or Dad again throughout the ten years I was away at school, nor for decades afterwards.

It would take nearly fifty years before I switched that emotion chip on again, before I let my shields come down once more. Until then I boarded up my heart and detached myself emotionally. I dissociated from my circumstances and, at 8 years old, became a fractured human being.

LIGHTS OUT

A friend of mine in New Zealand, who has spent much of his life giving pastoral care to help people into wholeness, recently shared this in a written message:

> One English guy said to me once that for the first two weeks he was at boarding school – he went when he was just 7 years old – when the lights were turned out in the dormitory at night, all you could hear was little boys crying.

A few sentences later, he made this remark:

> The great English mountaineer, Chris Bonnington, wrote in a book of his that I have, that when you are in a tight spot in the mountains, the best person to have with you is a Brit! The reason: Brits will never face critical situations with any emotion.

How is it that the same little boys who cried themselves to sleep at boarding school become these men who face crises without emotions?

Here we must return to the cycle of pain. After the experience of desertion by their parents and the dawning realization of the deprivations they now suffer in a place of privilege, girls and boys are faced with one of two choices: either they implode emotionally and leave, or they shut down their emotions and stay. The vast majority choose the latter. They detach themselves from the privations that they now endure. In the process, the thinking side of their souls begins to dominate, leaving the feelings behind. 'This is going to be good for me, however much it hurts,' is the message that the mind believes. Meanwhile, the feelings of abandonment are subjugated underneath the legitimizing narrative that both their parents and the institution reinforce.

THE VOW OF DETACHMENT

The response to the loss of attachment with one's parents is what I call the 'vow of detachment'. The boy or girl, shocked by the realization that they are separated from their parents' love, reacts by subordinating their emotions to their intellects. This is exactly what the boarding school system in a sense needs. If boarding school is the stepping stone to universities like Cambridge and Oxford, then by its very nature it must nurture thinkers. The more a child learns to rationalize, the more they ready themselves for the academic rigours of the journey. Whether boarding schools admit it or not, whether they are even aware of it or not, the fact is that the boarder's choice to disengage emotionally and to live within the mind is precisely the kind of decision that the system needs, not just to survive but to thrive. If academic success is the goal – a success judged by how many boys and girls gain 'A' grades at A Level and entrance to the most prestigious universities – then it is actually beneficial to the boarding school system for boys and girls to become more cerebral and less emotional. Whether it is beneficial to the boys and girls involved . . . that – to quote Hamlet – is the question.

I'm in no doubt that at both my boarding schools this argument would have provoked objections. 'Our aim is to provide a well-rounded education,' was the common cry. However, the words 'well rounded' are justified when applied to the *content* of the education. I did indeed receive training in a diversity of areas. I developed into a person who was capable both at academic studies and at sport. But they are not justified when applied to the *recipients* of the education. I didn't become a 'well-rounded person.' Like countless others, I separated mind and heart and chose to live within the former for nearly five decades of my life, to the cost of my former marriage and my family.

The harsh reality is this: at some stage, at the age of 8 or 9 (sometimes later too), the boarder makes a kind of inner vow. Whether they are conscious of this or not is debatable. Whether they articulate it or not is doubtful. But somewhere in the soul, the boarder makes a decision to keep their real feelings hidden and to maintain a stiff upper lip. They make an inner commitment to disengage their feelings and to shut down. This vow of detachment is like a monastic vow of silence. It is not just made by one boarder, it is made collectively – maybe not at the same moment, as in some formal rite of initiation, but certainly unconsciously. At this point the crying stops – like the taps in the white-walled bathrooms before lights out.

Two fractures occur within the soul whenever this occurs: the first we've discussed. It is between thoughts and feelings, intellect and emotions, the mind and the heart. From this moment on, the child lives with a boarded heart. This is the only way that they can manage their homesick souls. But this is not the only consequence. A second disintegration now occurs, between the private and the public. Privately the child may be suffering but publicly she or he employs a different narrative. As psychiatrist Piers Partridge said on the BBC's *The Making of Them*:

> If I'd been asked aged 9 or 10 how I was doing, what I would have said was, 'Well, I was homesick at first but I've settled down quite a lot now, thank you. You can't be attached to your Mum's apron strings forever, you know. I feel much happier now here and it's jolly good fun in the dorms, you know.' You learned to be who you knew you had to be and you had to be a good chap, to be getting on with it and be part of the system. That's what I learned to do. But I went on missing my home terribly.

NO MORE VULNERABILITY

The decision to disengage emotions at boarding school has lifelong consequences. In particular, it results in two tendencies that are massively detrimental to the human soul. The first is the rejection of vulnerability in oneself; the second is the rejection of vulnerability in others.

One ex-boarder, reviewing documentary *The Making of Them*, as well as their experience of being sent away to school, wrote this:

> What I remember most from that time in my life is the intense loneliness, the homesickness, the sense of alienation and difference from all the other boys. In retrospect, much later, I learned to acknowledge that I was suffering but would have been unable to formulate such a realization at the time. As an act of self-preservation, if nothing else, it was necessary to conceal it. Vulnerability was not an option. I created for myself a fine, extremely effective coat of

armour – and wore it for another four decades. I still find myself, today, shielding myself from the unkind world out there! I am still uncomfortable with my body. I still 'hold myself in'.[19]

Did you notice what the man said? 'Vulnerability was not an option.' In other words, boys and girls at boarding school choose to conceal rather than reveal their true feelings. They hide, as orphans always do, choosing to live a life of secrecy, cowering behind a public mask – an iron mask no less, forged on the anvil of their boarding institutions. They decide that their feelings of rejection and abandonment must not be owned. These strong emotions must be held in chains in the shadow lands of the human soul. They must never be allowed to surface from these subterranean depths. Big boys and girls don't cry. They simply carry on. They are survivors.

If the first consequence of the vow of detachment is the rejection of vulnerability in oneself, the second is the rejection of vulnerability in others. No one has articulated this more honestly than the man I quoted just now, for whom vulnerability was not an option. Reviewing the BBC documentary, he gave voice to the disapproval he felt towards the grown up men revealing how their boarding schools had wounded them:

> I'll confess to a part of myself that listened to the grown men in this powerful and moving documentary . . . with the knee-jerk response: they're 'wet', to resort to the boys' school terminology; they're 'pathetic'. These extraordinarily privileged men actually feel sorry for themselves. Such was my conditioned reaction; and in this way was my conditioning so powerful, it triggered that judgement over

decades of sometimes deep inner work and reflection. Because I recognized myself in them, these men who had come to understand the depth of the wound they had sustained, and the lasting effects it can have on a man's life – including, but not limited to the ability to form trusting relationships and engage in simple expressions of love. Like the hugs my wife reminds me again this morning, as I write, I am too reticent to share.[20]

See how the rejection of vulnerability is not just applied by ex-boarders to themselves. It is applied to others too, in particular to those who start being honest. The problem with this is of course that the rejection of vulnerability leads to an outright refusal to deal with the vulnerability of rejection. While a person lives with this rejection, the soul remains disintegrated and the person lives forever in the half-light of survival rather than the bright light of a life well lived. The wound must be faced head on. Feeling rejected by one's parents is a trauma whose shockwaves reverberate in the soul for generations, sometimes to the very point of death.

ATTACHMENT IS FAILURE

What happens to a boy or girl who makes this choice to detach their feelings in their childhood? The answer is, they begin to believe lies about life and about themselves. These lies function as toxic beliefs. They are the tenets of the boarded heart – the creed of the homesick soul.

One of these lies is that 'attachment is failure'. If a boy or a girl admits to their love for their parents, and the fact that they miss them terribly, that is seen as weakness. As Piers Partridge said on the BBC documentary:

> Anybody who knows a 7-year-old or an 8-year-old knows that they are attached to their parents, and attached to the places they live, and that there's nothing wrong with that. It's human. To grow up in an environment where you consider that to be a failure, of course that has an impact on your adult life.

What happens to a child when they grow up believing this lie about human attachments? The consequences, as Piers explained, are devastating:

> You grow up after ten years of that experience deeply believing that it is a failure to have feelings about being attached to another adult that you love. When you're then growing up and you're in your thirties and your forties, and you're trying to form relationships, a close intimate relationship with someone else, that is a great mountain to climb, to believe that it's going to be okay to get that close to a human being again.

A boarding school education therefore comes at a great price. Yes, that price is in part financial. The sacrifices made in monetary terms are huge. But the biggest price is relational. Men and women with boarded hearts find it hard to have close, intimate relationships.

Chris Baker, who was a prep-school boarder between 1968 and 1972 (exactly the same years as mine), said this in the documentary:

My parents said they sent me there because they loved me and because they wanted the best possible education for me and the school also said that it was a privilege to be there but although I was told these things the effect was that I was actually pushed away and rejected by my parents. Still now, when people say they love me, or they like me, I get the sense of distrust and fear that they're going to reject me and push me out.

This is by no means an isolated case. It is now a well-documented fact that many ex-boarders find it hard to have long marriages and happy, functional families. Having shut down their emotions at an early age, intimacy is a problem, to put it mildly. Having repressed their sexuality as something 'forbidden', they are handicapped from experiencing a long and healthy sexual relationship. Is it any wonder that there are so many spouses of ex-boarders, either hanging on or now divorced, who have suffered from a lack of intimacy from their marriage partner? Is it any wonder that there are so many children of ex-boarders who have suffered from a lack of emotional engagement from their mums or dads (or both)?

WHEN ED MET SU

Let me paint a picture in story form that illustrates the point.

Ed is a fictional construct. His name 'ED' stands for Emotionally Disengaged. He goes to prep and public school, starting at the age of 7. He is traumatized by his separation from his mum and dad and chooses to become a survivor. Surviving means becoming emotionally disconnected.

Su is also a fictional construct. Her name 'SU' stands for

Sexually Underdeveloped. Her public school experience, from the age of 13 to 18, coincides with her puberty. Her boarding house is run by a housemistress, a religious woman who has never married. The message that the girls receive is that all flesh must be covered up and that kissing boys beyond the ancient walls is utterly forbidden. A religious undertone accompanies this message, that sex is dirty, even within marriage.

Ed and Su meet at Oxbridge University. They go to the same college and they study the same subject. In a tutorial one day, Ed invites Su to a local Greek restaurant and the two begin to fall in love. Before long, they are both entwined. Ed loves sex. It is the closest thing he knows to intimacy. Su loves it too, at least for now, because it is forbidden.

The two get wed, but from day one they begin to drift apart. Ed, who is emotionally disengaged, does not know how to reveal the face behind his mask. He has learned so well to conceal his orphaned heart that he cannot bring himself to let Su into the caverns of his soul where grief and rage cohabit. She wants him to but he cannot. He trusted his parents but they deserted him. What if he trusts Su? Will she abandon him as well?

Su, meanwhile, has undergone a subtle, quiet revolution in her soul. Until the moment when the knot was tied, sex with Ed was quite intoxicating, fuelled as it was by the thought of its illicitness. Sex is the forbidden fruit and she has tasted eagerly of its flesh. Now, however, she is married and it is legal. Sex has lost its fiery allure. Its dirtiness impresses and distresses her. For her it is another chore, another act of clearing up Ed's mess, another duty to perform, another sacrifice.

Not long afterwards, Su becomes pregnant and they

have twins. As the son and daughter occupy Su's world, the abandonment that Ed had felt at 7 years old begins to pull upon his soul, especially now that their sex life is no longer passionate but perfunctory. Ed looks with secret jealousy at Su's soothing, nurturing affection for their children. He doesn't realize how much he's missed a mother's arms, right from the moment when his mother left him at the entrance of his school. He longs to be mothered so, but Su can never fill the mother-shaped void in his life. If he makes her try, she will never meet that need and he will stay emotionally stunted.

As Ed descends into an inner world of anger and frustration, Su's frustration escalates as well. She now laments Ed's lack of engagement in her world and even begs him at one point, 'Shout at me! Hit me! Anything, Ed. Anything to show me that you feel!' When the twins reach the age of 7, something now shifts within Ed's fractured soul. He is not aware of it at all but this is the age at which he chose to disengage and turn into a survivor when he went away to school. This was the age at which he learned to live independently from his parents. Unconsciously, he disengages emotionally from his kids, believing the lie that they need to stand on their own two feet as he had done.

Su makes the opposite choice. Her maternal instincts trump her boarding school pain and she carries on playing the bigger part, listening to her children as they make their way into their teens. By now Ed's working life is fulfilling him. He is in leadership in a thriving company. Money is no longer short. Things are going well. Ed is in demand both in the UK and abroad. He travels often, near and far, leaving Su to hold the reins.

At some point in this timeframe, the differences between Ed

and Su begin to morph from manageable to irreconcilable. As the kids move into their twenties, Ed and Su are separated and then divorced.

Ed begins to recognize that while he has succeeded in his work, he has failed in the two areas where he wanted to succeed the most: as husband and as dad. He detaches himself emotionally even more. This is the only way he knows how to survive. He learned the tactic early on in life.

Su is left confused and angry. In her mind, she has done everything to keep the family together. She knows she hasn't met Ed's needs. How could she? He's not in touch with what he really needs himself.

The twins meanwhile are devastated too. Their father wasn't there for them while he was present. Now he is absent physically as well as emotionally. Their pain is indescribable, their anger unimaginable.

And so the story ends.

Or does it?

THE TERROR OF ABANDONMENT

This may just be a fiction but I guarantee that there are many reading it who say, 'The details may not be the same, but the storyline is one with which I'm intimately familiar.' Somewhere, deep within your soul, you may be saying. 'Boarding school is where I learned to be like this.'

There is a massive price to shutting down at boarding school, whether this applies to shutting down emotionally or shutting down sexually. The legacy of broken marriages and homes is ample evidence.

A lady whom I've known for nearly twenty years wrote just last week to me. I hadn't known why it was she wasn't married any more, and had never asked. But hearing that I was writing this book, she sent me a brief but telling private message on Facebook:

> It is not just the boarders who have hurts to heal but also those who have tried to love them. My ex was sent back to England from Africa at the age of 6 by his missionary parents. He was sent to boarding school and didn't see his parents again for six years. His problems with abandonment, rejection, lack of love and the belief that the service of God was more important to his parents than love for their children, crippled our marriage. Eventually he left home rather than continue with the constant fear that I would one day abandon him too.

Another woman wrote to me about a broken engagement:

> I once lost a fiancé because he honestly felt that I was someone who wanted to be loved, and because of his boarding school experience, he was incapable of ever loving anyone. He was so messed up. He wanted to love and be loved but he didn't know how to do either, so he ran.

And so he ran.

Why is it that we ex-boarders run? What is it that drives us to flee from intimacy and authentic relationships, especially within marriage? I'll tell you. It is fear and fear is the natural offspring of shame. Shame says, 'I know in my head that my parents loved me and wanted the best for me, but I can't help feeling deep down that there was something wrong with me.' A person feeling this way is bound to be afraid of ever feeling this way again.

SHAME, FEAR AND CONTROL

Shame, as I've already indicated, is the deep-rooted and debilitating sense of one's own unworthiness. In relation to boarding school pain, shame is the corrosive lie in the soul that says, 'They left me there because there was something defective about me.' If a child was sent away because they were naughty or unmanageable at home, or at a day school, then this feeling will be even more destructive. The child may well believe the lie that they were bad or 'not good enough' for the rest of their lives. They may struggle with depression, trying desperately to unseat the wicked witch of shame that sits and snipes at them upon the throne of their emotions.

If this shame is left unrecognized and untreated, the child grows up with one great fear within their heart – the fear of being left alone, left behind, again. When a child grows up still bound by terrors such as these, they enter marriage with needs their partners simply cannot meet. Terrified by the imagined prospect of a further exile, such men and women drive their feelings even further underground, seeking to master their fears by controlling their emotions and, worse still, controlling other people and controlling their relationships. In the end, they may well abandon those they love because they'd rather do it to another than ever have it done again to them.

What we are talking about here is a classic psychological process or pattern:

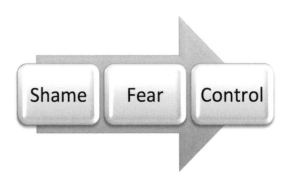

The narrative goes something like this.

If I feel ashamed as a result of being separated from my parents' love, I may well be afraid – afraid of any further separations in my life. The shame of being left alone results in a fear of experiencing anything like it ever again. This fear may be buried deep but the person living with it feels the vibrations of what is called 'separation anxiety' all the time, like a background noise that never goes away. The victim, desperate to remove this dread, resorts to controlling not just their emotions but their relationships. At home they control the ones they love and hope that in the process this will build a sure defence against abandonment. At work they control their colleagues in the hope that they will build a wall against redundancy, so that they will never be abandoned by the institution that has come to be another parent figure in their lives. This strategy, however, does not always work.

CLARKSON'S RAGE

In 2015, after his now infamous incident punching a BBC producer, *Top Gear* presenter Jeremy Clarkson began to talk about his years at boarding school. The version in the *Independent* ran with the following headline: 'Jeremy Clarkson says he was bullied at public school: 'I was made to lick the lavatories clean and boys defecated in my tuck box.'[21] Recounting his experiences in the 1970s, Clarkson confessed to having been subjected to 'all the usual humiliations that public school used back then to turn a small boy into a gibbering, sobbing, suicidal wreck'. He added, 'I was thrown on an hourly basis into the icy plunge pool, dragged from my bed in the middle of the night and beaten.' This started when he arrived at his public school, and then became progressively worse throughout the following years.

The one thing that Clarkson treasured most was the Omega watch his father had given him before he left for boarding school. 'In the first two years the older boys broke pretty much everything I owned. They glued my records together, snapped my compass, ate my biscuits, defecated in my tuck box and cut my trousers in half with a pair of garden shears, but I made sure when I heard them coming that my watch was safely locked away.' That watch has become a symbol of survival. Sometimes he still takes it out to 'wind it up and remind myself that no matter how awful life might be, it was, from 1973 to 1975, one hell of a lot worse.'

Even granted the usual Clarkson hyperbole, this is a grim reminder of the effect of bullying in boarding school. As if it was not enough to have suffered the shame of being exiled from their home, boarders often have to suffer the further agony of humiliation by bullies operating covertly within their boarding houses. This creates an agonizing cocktail. On top of the shame of abandonment are added measures of the shame of abuse. How does a boy or a girl endure this?

The answer is, by shutting down. The boarder boards up their heart. They push the weeping and the rage right down as far as it will go, repressing it for years until one day an unsuspecting colleague in the workplace, or loved one in the home, applies some pressure to the wound. Then the anger rises up, like lava from the mouth of a volcano, to scorch and scar the innocent.

This is the survival strategy of those who go to boarding school. They shut down their emotions. Their grief and rage against the injustices of abandonment and abuse lie low within the soul. Sometimes these strong emotions never surface, even to the point of death.

CASTAWAYS AT SCHOOL

You see now why those who have been away to school construct a boarded heart? They are, deep down, terrified of being alone again, left behind to face a further dose of shame. They are terrified, in short, of rejection and abandonment.

What is the difference between rejection and abandonment? The difference is that rejection is malevolent. When a parent comes to hate their child and wants to send them away to school, this is rejection. Whatever the parents' motives, if this act of sending their child to boarding school is done with a wilful longing to be rid of them, then that is rejection. To reject someone, as the Latin root suggests, is to cast someone away.

This kind of separation is devastating. The child, convinced that they have been expelled from home, may now repeat this pattern over and over again, being expelled from one school after another, from one job after another in adult life. Convinced that they are only worthy of being rejected, the individual constantly replays the narrative. Even though they're terrified of being pushed away, they seem to cause the very thing they hate and say like Job, again and again, 'What I feared has come upon me' (Job 3:25).

Rejection, accordingly, is deliberate and malevolent.

Abandonment, on the other hand, is neither wilful nor malicious. A parent may leave their children in the hands of an institution, such as an orphanage or boarding school, because they honestly believe that they will have a better chance in life than if they stayed with them. When a child is left for benevolent reasons, this is abandonment.

This is what happened in relation to my birth mother. She believed that Claire and I would have a greater opportunity to make it if she left us, in the early sixties, with some nuns in London – a story line I see repeated time again on the TV show *Call the Midwife*.

This is also what happened in relation to my adoptive parents. They believed that Claire, Giles and I would have a better education and thus better opportunities in life if they left us all at boarding school. In both cases, the effect was to feel abandoned but not rejected.

If rejection is malevolent, abandonment is more benevolent, at least from the parental perspective. The parents' motives, if they reject their child, are cruel. Their motives, if they abandon them, are not. Whether their motives are cruel or kind, in shutting down at school, and then in later life in grown-up interactions, the child decides to drown out all their fears of feeling abandoned or rejected ever again. They have become castaways once. They never want to feel cast away again.

COMPLETE CONTROL

The fear of separation, whether this separation takes the form of rejection or abandonment, is what leads the child to shut down, not just at school but often in the contexts they inhabit afterwards as well. Shame leads to fear and fear leads to control. This first manifests itself as *self*-control. The boarder learns from early on that self-control is valuable. Mastering one's passions – that ancient Roman virtue of the 'manly man' – is what matters most in life. Vulnerability is the very opposite of what it means to be a woman or a man. 'Control yourself' is the lesson taught by schools, backed up cleverly by lessons from philosophy and literature, recreation and religion.

The trouble with this is that vulnerability is the path to wholeness at every level of our lives. Admitting that you're wounded is not weakness – it is strength. It is not cowardice – it is courage. As I've said a thousand times, 'If you don't get real, you don't get healed.' Pushing down your hurts beneath a boarded heart is the very opposite of health. It is also the very opposite of sanity. Anyone who has had even a smattering of learning from psychology knows this. Sharing your story of shame is the pathway to finding freedom from the chains that bind you. As long as you repress your feelings, shame grows stronger by the day.

The second way control is manifested is with others.

I remember fondly the French teacher at my public school. We had to sit in booths with headsets on and practise saying words and phrases after him. He was an old, eccentric Russian man, who would wait until we were all sitting down, our microphones and headsets at the ready. He would then turn on the master switch and say, 'And now I am in *complete* control.'

For ex-boarders, control is a massive issue. Not only do we have to be in complete control of our emotions, keeping them in check. We have to be in complete control of others, keeping them far away enough that we will never again be hurt as we were so deeply all those years ago when Mum and Dad drove off and left us all alone. Is it any wonder that ex-boarders make such great recruits for MI5 and MI6? They know how to control themselves. They know how to acquire information. Add to this their undying loyalty to the 'parent institution' and you have the perfect mix of qualities for British secret agents in the field. Indeed, I sometimes wonder what would ever happen to our Secret Service if the boarding system stopped!

The Survivor Mindset

Shutting down is therefore the main consequence of boarding school. It may not be everyone's story. There are some who regard it as the happiest days of their lives. Whether they are in denial or not, I do not know. All I can say is that my experience and that of many others, is that the only way we endured the exile from our homes was to create a boarded heart. We turned off our emotion chips and learned somehow to survive.

Is it any surprise ex-boarders cope so well with further deprivations in their lives? My father, for example, went to fight against the Japanese as part of Wingate's Army. He fought behind the enemy lines until one day he was severely wounded. A Gurkha soldier called Moto fended for him in the jungle, until one day the rifleman was caught, interrogated and shot.

My father was then found and taken to a prison camp. For

three years, he suffered terribly as a prisoner of war, surviving somehow by reciting lines he'd learned at school and university – Milton, Wordsworth and many others. Then he was liberated and brought home.

At this point, some may say, 'Shutting down was beneficial. Your father would have never made it had he not detached himself from all the awful things around him.' That is undoubtedly true. In the right context, shutting down can indeed be helpful, helping you to endure what otherwise would overwhelm you.

But in the wrong context, it is not.

I remember many times as I went through my teens when Mum would start to shout. Dad would be there, along with all three of us children. Mum, who by this stage had been diagnosed with depression, would lose it and start screaming, sometimes even showing signs of impending violence. As children, we would look at Dad and see the same thing every time. He'd bow his head and look away. He simply wasn't there. He had turned his emotions off. This may have worked for him but it didn't work for us. The less he was engaged, the more my mother was enraged.

One day I asked him why he did this.

'When the Japanese NCO used to scream at us POWS,' he answered, 'it was imperative you didn't look at him. You had to look away and somehow disengage. Your ability to do that was the difference between being beaten or not – sometimes between being beheaded or not.'

And then he paused before saying, 'I suppose I'm just reacting the same way when Mum explodes.'

LIGHTS ON

This is the dilemma of the boarded heart. Yes, there are moments when shutting down is right. But not every situation demands this conscious strategy of detachment. In relationships it's vital to be emotionally engaged. Men and women need their spouses to look them in the eye and share what's going on behind that well-worn mask. They need their spouses to lower their shields and remove the armour around their soul. If they do not, this will rob the marriage of its intimacy.

Children need this too. They need their mums and dads to engage with them emotionally. They need eye contact, undistracted attention, even empathy. Without them the child will feel that same separation from a parent's love that the parent felt when he or she was left alone by Mum and Dad all those years ago. Unless ex-boarders learn to reengage emotionally with life, they will always live in a world of paradoxes. They will live in the land of plenty at work while living in a land of poverty at home.

This was my story for many years.

It is many people's story, both men and women.

Sooner or later we have to emerge from underneath the covers of our dormitory beds and reveal our true selves to the ones we love.

Sooner or later, we have to turn the lights back on.

5. COMFORTABLY NUMB

Sometime around the age of 9 or 10, I was playing in a football (soccer) match out on a windswept pitch at my prep school. At the time I was not at all enamoured with 'games' as they were called. The idea of putting on shorts and marching out onto a muddy field and dripping in the driving, winter rain was the very opposite of my idea of fun. On this particular day, during this particular game, I was not in the mood for a mud bath followed by cold, communal showers.

My attitude deteriorated even more when the goalkeeper on our team was injured and the referee nominated me to take his place.

'But sir, I've never played in goal.'

'Do as you're told, Stibbe.'

I replaced my blue team shirt with a lurid yellow jersey and trundled to the centre of the goal.

Within a minute, the opposition's centre forward charged into our penalty box. He was about to rocket the ball in my direction when a gangly centre back stretched out his long leg and felled the boy.

The whistle went immediately.

'Penalty!' the referee shouted.

My heart sank. Everyone knew it was a cast iron certainty that the boy, now positioning the ball meticulously upon the chalky remnants that once had been the penalty spot, would send the ball into the back of the net.

The whistle blew again.

The cocky boy began his run up.

At that moment something utterly unexpected occurred. Something I had no idea I had – call it basic intuition – took control and I found myself flying through the air towards the left-hand post. The ball, which the boy had kicked perfectly, was heading fast into the top corner of the goal. Just before it crossed the line and filled the trembling net, my hands reached behind the ball. Not only did I stop it. I caught it too!

Landing in the goal mouth, I stood up with the ball clasped, like some priceless treasure, to my chest and stood there, nonchalant and confident, as if I'd saved such efforts many times before.

There was a gasp.

Then some cheers.

And finally, a ripple of applause broke not only from the boys but also from the referee.

That moment changed my boarding life. The thrill I felt at doing the impossible and the buzz I received from the approval of my peers was utterly intoxicating. From that time on, I lived for repetitions of that moment, driving myself beyond the call of duty, braving the most inclement weather in extra practices and training, working my way up the school teams until at last I managed to become the goalkeeper in the first eleven in both my prep and public schools. By 16, I was being invited to have trials with what we would today call a Premier League club. It was exhilarating.

Looking for an Anaesthetic

Am I sharing this to boast? Maybe a little, but the main reason is to highlight something that I feel the recent literature on boarding school does not address. I'm talking here about addiction. Addiction is a process in which you gradually hand over the control of your life to a substance, behaviour, relationship or belief on which you fix your absolute attention. These substances, behaviours, relationships and beliefs become your idol, the focus of an all-consuming worship. Their power consists in this, that for a moment what they offer masks the pain that nothing else can touch. They act as anaesthetics, numbing the gnawing ache within the soul, the longing and the deep desire for love. The problem with such obsessive and compulsive cravings is they never ultimately remove the pain. In fact, they leave a person emptier than they were before because the relief they offer is only ever transient.

What happens to this pain that boarders feel? They may shut down emotions, as we have seen, but is this disengagement the only strategy they adopt when separated from their parents' love?

The answer is no.

In addition to the detaching of emotions, the boarder typically embraces dependencies or attachments. These function as a compensation for the loss of healthy attachment to their mothers and their fathers. The process therefore looks something like this: the loss of healthy attachment to one's parents results in emotional detachment. This emotional detachment is insufficient on its own to mask the pain, so the boarded heart looks round for pain-relieving attachments that will give a semblance of the affirmation and approval they have lost in being exiled from their home.

In other words, boarders do two things.

First, they intellectualize their pain. They repeat the mantra they were taught. 'This is the making of me,' they say. 'Everyone else is going through this, so I will too. I just need to keep a stiff upper lip.'

However, this, on its own, is not enough. So the boarder resorts to a second approach. They don't just intellectualize their pain. They anaesthetize it too. They look for dependencies that will act as substitute affections.

The Allure of Food

What kinds of substitutes are on offer at a typical prep or public school? The answer is 'many'. My drug of choice at prep school was football. Once I had experienced the high of the adulation of my peers, I was hooked. I worked as hard as I could do to recreate the narcotic rush of the approval and applause of others in my school. I went well beyond what others did to make that thrill a possibility. In the absence of the affirmation and approval of my absent parents, I found a substitute in sport. Nothing could compare with the adulation of a line or two of boys applauding on the touchline of a match where I was flying, Bonetti-like, through the air. It was addictive.

By the time I moved to public school, around my thirteenth birthday, I had begun to find some other anaesthetics for my soul. The first of these was food. Eating became a substitute for love.

One of my most vivid memories at public school was ending lessons at nearly 6 p.m. and rushing with my straw hat tilting on my head back to the boarding house. The idea was to get as close to the head of the table in the dining hall as possible. Those at the head got first dibs at the grub.

This was especially important on a Friday. Friday evening, Fred our chef served fish and chips, sausage and chips, or egg and chips. If you got delayed at school, you would likely find yourself at the end of the table. This was nothing short of disastrous! Often you received the sorry remnants.

I learned early on that the key was to get back to the dining hall as quickly as possible and to eat your food as fast as you could. That way you could (a) get as much as possible, and (b) stand a good chance of having seconds. In a community where every boy discovered this, the consequences were of course chaotic. I don't think any of us ever ran as fast on tracks or pitches as we did the cobbled quads and gravel paths back to the dining hall. As soon as the bell sounded for the end of the day, we bolted from the classrooms like greyhounds pelting after some bedraggled hare.

Looking back, I now believe that this was more than just a hungry teen trying to fill the bottomless pit of my stomach. It has taken me nearly fifty years to recognize that the habits I formed and learned at boarding school were strategies not only of survival but of attachment too. I have to watch myself, even to this day. In my worst moments, I still want to be the first at any table. I still want to fill my plate up full, whether others fill their plates or not. I now see this as a false, unhealthy attachment – as the conduct of an unhealed, orphaned heart, not the pattern of a healthy soul.

Many days at public school, I found my way down to the junior common room where I could purchase meals and sweets. I'd buy beans on toast and a bowl of chips, douse them in tomato ketchup and consume them at a breakneck speed. Then a short while later I'd have my evening meal in the boarding house, then buttered toast before bed.

The only reason I wasn't the size of a small zeppelin was because I was addicted to sport as well!

Today I wonder how much my attitude towards food and eating was shaped by experiences at boarding school. How many of us later in life have struggled with eating disorders of one kind or another because we learned to use food as a substitute for love at boarding school? How many of us have struggled with addiction to alcohol or drugs (either legal or illegal) because we used these as substitutes for the attachments that we missed at home? Would we have eaten in the way we have if we had been at home, dining with our families? Would we have drunk vast quantities of alcohol had we grown up in environments where alcohol was introduced more sensibly and monitored more lovingly? Would we have resorted to mood-altering drugs had we traversed the road from childhood to our adulthood in contexts where there was little separation from a parent's love?

Maybe I am idealizing the experience of growing up at home but I have an inkling things are different for those who come back home from school at 4 p.m. I look wistfully at TV shows like the celebrated *The Royle Family*, where children grow to adults within families that stay together. They may be broke and far from perfect but they are at least together.

INTELLECTUAL ADDICTIONS

The second drug I found was in academic performance. I quickly came to the rather prudent conclusion that at A levels and beyond the secret was to find the one thing I was good at and exploit that to the full. That one thing was English literature. I loved reading and writing poetry. I loved listening to teachers expounding what great writing meant. It energised me.

There was an English teacher at my public school whose expertise was unparalleled. He was possibly the most brilliant person I have ever met and the only one to fully understand my favourite poet, Wallace Stevens. I would sit enthralled listening to him taking hold of complex lines and unravelling them. His teaching mesmerized me – both the content and the method. He was breathtakingly brilliant.

My dream became to emulate this man of letters so I did with literature what I had done with football. I went the extra mile. I read and read and I wrote and wrote. One night I stayed up until 3 a.m. filling twelve A4 sheets with my thoughts, written in ink, in the same handwriting style as my teacher whom I idolized. It was an essay on *Paradise Lost* and it was one I had written voluntarily, not as a course requirement.

When my teacher returned it, there were no red marks anywhere in the text, just a simple statement at the end – A+++, outstanding. When I read that, I was back again at prep school on the playing field, receiving the approval and the affirmation that I craved.

From that moment on, I sought to maximize my one and only academic talent. My passion grew and grew, not just for the subject but also for the approval I had felt. My nickname became 'Plato' because I was constantly quoting him, even though I was not required to study any of his writings at the time. By the end of my time at school, I had worked so hard I had a chance of getting into Cambridge University. When the phone call came from the admissions tutor, I was at home and my whole family was waiting outside my father's study to hear what news had come.

'I've been awarded an exhibition to read English at Trinity,' I said. My father, who was standing on the stairs outside the room, sat down.

According to my brother who was next to him, he cried.

That night I received affirmation and approval from the ones I'd missed for over a decade – my father and my mother.

CREATING A FALSE SELF

All this shows, however anecdotally, that the boarder has at least two strategies at school. These can be summarized as:

INTELLECTUALIZING
- Unhealthy Detachment

ANAESTHETIZING
- Unhealthy Attachment

When it comes to the anaesthetizing tendency, this can take many forms: it can consist of over-attachment to eating, drinking, taking drugs, forming addictive relationships, sex, work, money, technology, beliefs, sport, whatever masks the pain of being separated from parental love. The problem with resorting to obsessive attachments to these things is not just the fact their pain relief is temporary; it is also that they lead us to construct a version of ourselves that may not be true to who we are – that may in fact be an entirely mythical creation, born out of the need to make it through a decade where it's the fittest who survive, born out of a need for approval.

For Eric Idle, one of the great talents in the Monty Python team, the mask he forged was a comic one. He learned, in effect, to play the fool at boarding school. He discovered he could make his peers and others laugh. This was the one thing he could do, at least from his perspective. So he squeezed every drop he could from this gift. The laughter he elicited was his drug of choice. Comedy, as he put it, became his survival gene.

There are therefore two great problems with the anaesthetizing tendency and both have to do with the word 'mask'. The first is that over-attachment to the addictive items I have mentioned here cannot completely and effectively mask the pain within. The second is that these unhealthy attachments lead a person to wear a mask – the mask of the comedian, the sportsman, the intellectual, or the anarchist. This mask may cover who we truly are.

Indeed, an ex-boarder may never fully meet and embrace their true self. They may live for the rest of their lives out of the false self they constructed at their boarding school as part of their survival kit.

GREAT EXPECTATIONS

What happens to men and women who go through years and years of such detachment and dependency? The answer cannot be given in a simple, single sound bite. The truth is there are many consequences. Perhaps the most debilitating legacy occurs in those who feel they've failed, who feel they haven't measured up to the dreams their parents had for them, who didn't repay the sacrifices made financially. This sense of being a disappointment to their parents can crush a boy or girl of 18 or 19 years of age. Shame is piled on shame with sometimes devastating effects.

My best friend at public school was called Billy (not his real name). Tall, good-looking, kind, and extremely witty, Billy was a cheery-eyed and loyal ally through public school. When we left, I went on to read English Literature at Cambridge while he chose to go to another university to study English Literature and Film. This was one of the few places in the UK where the study of film was offered as a genuine, academic degree-level course. I remember being very jealous. Billy and I loved films. My fondest memory of our friendship was when he somehow managed to acquire a reel of the first *Star Wars* movie before it went on general release. He set up his Super 8 projector, and late one night we watched Princess Leia walking on the wall of his study. I don't think I have ever fully recovered!

We lost touch a little after that, as is so often the case with friendships made at boarding school.

The next I heard was sometime later, around the middle of our second year at university. Billy's father, a hugely influential man and a knight of the realm, asked me to phone him on an urgent matter.

'I'm afraid I have distressing news.'

My heart sank.

'Billy was found yesterday afternoon with his wrists slit.'

I gasped.

'Is he alive?'

'Yes, they found him just in time.'

'Where is he?'

'He's been moved from intensive care to another ward in the Norfolk and Norwich hospital.'

'I must see him,' I said.

' I'll drive up from London and give you a lift,' his father said.

When we visited Billy he was barely recognizable. He had completely shaved his head and was lying on a bed, his wrists bandaged. We spoke for a while, first with his father present, then on our own. It was not the most natural conversation in the world. Neither Billy nor I were used to going deeper than discussions of the latest films and football gossip. I knew he was hurting. I knew he was in great distress. But neither of us could bring ourselves to take away the masks and bare our souls.

Later that afternoon, as his father stepped into his car, he passed a photograph to me.

'Here,' he said. 'I found it in Billy's room.'

I looked at the picture. There were Billy's parents, his older brother – who had gone to Oxford University – his sister and his younger brother. In the centre, there was Billy. Only Billy's face was gone. He had taken a sharp knife, probably the one he used to cut himself, and left a perfect circle of white space where once his eyes and smile had been.

'What have I done to him?' the father asked.

'I don't know.'

But deep inside I think I did.

Billy felt like he had never measured up. Unlike his father and his older brother, he had not gone to Oxford University. He had not 'achieved' in his own eyes, at least not according to the unspoken values of his family and school, or of the legalistic religious group that he had joined. Devastated by a sense of shame – one his father never wanted him to feel – my friend had simply given up. Had it not been for a passing student – who noticed blood emerging underneath a toilet door – my friend surely would have died.

Today I cannot write these words without a sigh of sadness, not just for Billy, but for all those boys and girls fretting under 'great expectations'. Maybe, like Billy's parents, many dads and mums did not intend their offspring to cower under such a great and heavy weight. Maybe, like Billy's dad, they never wanted sons and daughters to seek their love and affirmation through excellent results and entrance to the so-called 'right' universities. Maybe they were and are enslaved within a pattern that is generational.

Whatever the case, dependency, when harnessed to detachment, has left an awful, inner legacy in many men and women through the years.

They may look confident and capable on the outside.

But on the inside, they're weeping.

THE DANGERS OF DEPENDENCY

What happens, then, to men and women who go through years and years of such detachment and dependency? The first answer is that they are robbed of life itself. Many live with a public face that's got it all together, while their private world is in ruins. They give the impression of living life to the max, but the reality is they are dying inside.

A second major consequence is that such men and women can be robbed of intimacy. Many go on from school to university and then from university to other institutions. They work long hours to gain yet more success while their home life suffers more and more.

Why does this happen?

One answer is because the former boarder does not recognize the depth of their detachment. Having taken out their emotion chip at school, they find it hard to express themselves with reality and depth and find it even harder to let others do the same. This robs both their spouse and their children of the precious gift of presence. The ex-boarder isn't present to their spouse or child. They may be generous, but what they never see is that presents are no substitute for presence. What the spouse or child desires is honesty and empathy. They long for the mask to come off and the real partner, the real parent, to appear. But that person disappeared a long, long time ago.

The other reason why such families are robbed of intimacy is because the former boarder does not recognize the depth of their dependency. Dependencies appear in many guises but supreme among them is an unhealthy attachment to achievement, arising from the performance ethos they grew up with in their boarding school. This leads to an intensely competitive mindset, born from an orphan-hearted need for missing affirmation and approval. This in turn results in overwork – in spending hours and hours in workplace slavery and living *for* approval rather than *from* approval.

The trouble with this kind of toxic attachment is that it has the same negative effects on a marriage and family as drug or alcohol addiction, both of which may sometimes accompany it.

In other words, it turns spouses into co-dependents.

The sad fact is that the spouse of a former boarder often

becomes involved in their dependency. They take on the role of a caretaker. If the former boarder is a man, the wife effectively becomes a mother not only to her children, but to her husband too. She is the one who finds that she is constantly covering for him and justifying his behaviour. Soon she learns not to say no to him. She does everything to make sure he is happy and that he can do what he must do. Meanwhile, she wonders where the love has gone. The children wonder where Dad has gone, too. The family has been robbed of intimacy.

I know that this is true.

It is not only the story of people I have met and counselled many times.

It is my story too.

WHERE HOPE IS BORN

However, the seeds for my recovery and eventual freedom were ironically planted in my public school experience.

One night in 1977, I was walking down a road called Kingsgate Street. At that time, a Christian revival had gripped the school and hundreds of boys had gone from being religiously apathetic or hostile into being committed, kind and altruistic Christians. This did not come through the chapel. As the headmaster at the time was later to record, the chapel's version of Christianity was all about being nice, and that had nothing to do with what had turned the world upside down two thousand years ago.[22] No, this was genuine, heartfelt, radical and vibrant Christianity – true to its Founder.

At the time, I was not into this at all but many of my friends had changed under its powerful influence, much to my displeasure. I was into sex, drugs, and rock and roll. I was into the philosophy of the existentialists, especially Albert Camus. I was into Pink Floyd and their album *The Wall*.

On that night in 1977, however, everything changed.

I was walking down the road and looking up at the stars. Inside I was singing the words of a song from *The Wall*, called 'Comfortably Numb'. Whilst I looked at the night sky, freckled by a thousand tiny lights, I sang a line from the song – 'Is there anybody out there?'

And suddenly, without any doubt, I knew there was.

That moment, the existential chill evaporated from my soul. I knew that I was not alone. I knew this orphaned planet had not been abandoned. I knew there was a God in heaven and I knew that through his Son he'd visited this cosmic orphanage and given us an invitation to return to him. He'd come looking for us and he was calling to us to come on home.

Suddenly I just knew that the answer to the hole in my soul was not a life of being comfortably numb. It was in my Heavenly Father's arms.

Whilst it would take me decades to understand the damage done by boarding school, the seeds of my freedom were sown in the soil of my heart right there and then, on the street whose name means 'the gate to the King'.

Like Scrooge, I had been visited by something from another world.

And like Scrooge, I had experienced an awakening.

PART 2: HOMECOMING

6. TELLING YOUR STORY

Like most people, my wife and I have a small collection of favourite films. One that has sentimental, if not cinematic, value is *Lady in the Water*.[23] It's not a masterpiece by any means, but it is a film we have watched more than once because it explores the healing power of story.

Lady in the Water tells of a man called Cleveland Heep, acted by Paul Giamatti. After a terrible tragedy, he retreats from his familiar world and becomes the handyman in a block of apartments. One day he discovers a beautiful girl in the swimming pool shared by people in the apartment complex. She appears as a water nymph and tells him that her name is 'Story', adding that she has come to find a man whose future book will enhance humankind. In seeking to find the author, Cleveland and Story are confronted by a sinister, lupine creature that not only seeks to destroy the mysterious writer but also Story herself, who is destined to be a great leader in her own world.

I won't tell you what happens to either Story or the mysterious writer but I will tell you what happens to Cleveland Heep. As he gets to know Story, his wounds begin to heal. She reads his journal when he is not looking and starts to help him confront his painful past:

'Your thoughts are very sad. Most are of one night. A night a man entered your home when you were not there. He stole many things and killed your wife and children. That is when you stopped being happy. You were a doctor. I am very sorry for you. You believe you have no purpose. You help all that live here.'

'Anybody can do this job, Story,' Cleveland replies.

'You have a purpose. All beings have a purpose.'

Cleveland starts to come to terms with the trauma of his loss. With Story's help, he begins to connect with his pain and, at a critical moment, he speaks as if his dead family were present.

'I'm sorry I couldn't protect you. Oh, I should have been there. I am always going to regret . . . just not being there. I'll miss your faces. They remind me of God. I'm so lost without you guys. I met this very nice lady, and her name's Story. I think you would have liked her. I think she might be . . . an angel, because she has to go home. I love you all. I love you all so much.'

As a result of his relationship with Story, Cleveland at last reconnects with his emotions and begins to let go of the terrible anguish and grief he has buried inside. At the end, he whispers to Story, 'Thank you for saving my life.'

Stories that Heal

I am not claiming that *Lady in the Water* is a great film, but it had a particularly powerful effect on me when I first saw it, for a number of reasons. One of these had to do with my growing sense of the healing power of story. I had spent much of my life up to that point studying stories and indeed telling stories. When I was in my late twenties, I completed a PhD on narrative theory and practice which was subsequently published by

Cambridge University Press.[24] My life since then has been given over to telling stories and empowering others to tell their stories. For me, story is what shapes our lives. Throughout our waking hours, we hear and share each other's stories. Even when we are asleep, our subconscious keeps on telling stories in the form of dreams. As human beings, we are defined and enhanced by story.

I am a firm believer that stories can be therapeutic – that they can be vehicles of healing. Like Cleveland Heep in the film, our lives may be broken. Our normal structures may have imploded all around and within us. We may be so numb that we cannot feel anything. But then a story begins to emerge from the shimmering blue waters between our conscious and subconscious minds. We start to own our story and share our story. Our past and present begin to take on a form, a meaning, a plot that gives us purpose – a sense that even in the wake of chaos and trauma there may be a reason not only for simply existing but for really living too.

Stories truly have the capacity to bring healing to our souls and they can do this in at least three ways. Firstly, when we own our story, share our story and learn to understand our story with the help of someone we trust, then we begin to find answers to the three most important questions a human being asks: Where have I come from? Who am I? What is my purpose and direction in life? These roughly correspond to the past, the present and the future. I summarize these three dimensions of existence with the letters H.I.D.

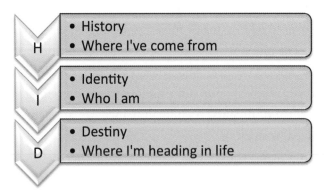

'H' stands for our history (the past tense of our story). 'I' stands for our identity (the present tense of our story). 'D' stands for our destiny (the future tense of our story). When we seek insight in the right places and from the right people, then what is H.I.D becomes disclosed. Our story is no longer concealed; our story is revealed and, in the process, we are healed.

The second way in which stories can become vehicles of healing is seen in the example from *The Lady in the Water*. Other people's stories – in this case, one written by Night Shyamalan – can sometimes have profound resonances with our own. When this happens, the story in question helps us to see our own suffering in a completely new light. It gives us keys which enable us to have our history healed, our identity sealed and our history revealed. When I began this book with *A Christmas Carol* and Scrooge's experience of abandonment at boarding school, this is exactly what I was seeking to do. Many people have said two things to me over the years about my use of this literary classic: firstly, that they have never seen the significance of this part of Dickens' story before and secondly, that it makes sense not only of Scrooge's story but their own. This is precisely what I mean by the healing power of stories. It's not just our own story that can become the vehicle for our recovery. Other peoples' stories, fiction or fact, can be instruments of recovery too.

Then there is a third way in which story can become a vehicle for our healing. This is when we start to see our own story in light of the overarching story of the oldest and most venerated story ever told: the Bible. The Bible is still the world's bestselling book. It is the fount of wisdom and meaning for over two billion people on our planet. It is the Father's story. It is the big story that can make sense of our little stories.

Stories of Homecoming

Why is the biblical story so critical in the healing process?

The answer is because the Bible addresses the core spiritual condition of every human being – the homesick soul. Every human being harbours an aching sense that they are somehow far away from home. At one time or another, we all feel as if we are in exile and that we are living on what I call 'an orphaned planet'. We all experience a spiritual version of what the psychologists call 'separation anxiety' – that fear of being left alone in an expanding universe. We know deep down that our attachment to the Love of all loves has been somehow broken and we live, as a result, with an existential dread, longing to be freed from our spiritual isolation and abandonment. In other words, we have homesick souls; like the prodigal son, we feel as if we are in the far country and we long to come home.

When we read the Bible relationally – as a love story – as opposed to religiously – as a law book – we begin to sense a stirring in our spirits. We sense that there is something altogether different about this book, that it tells a story which appeals to our need for homecoming. We have a deep presentiment that in these pages the answer to our alienation and aloneness in this cosmos can be found. As we begin to acknowledge our orphan state, that we are separated from our Father's love and full of shame, each page begins to take the form of a love letter from heaven, in which we hear the voice of the Father we've been waiting for – the Father who loves us like no earthly father or mother ever could, the One who promises never to leave us or abandon us. When this happens, and a silent 'yes' begins to rise from the trenches of our homesick souls, we have turned our face towards our heart's true home.

To summarize: there are therefore three ways in which healing can come to us in a story-shaped way.

Firstly, our own stories – once we own them and then begin to narrate them to trusted ones – will become the vehicles of healing to our boarded hearts as we confront the issues of our history, identity and destiny.

Secondly, other people's stories – whether they are the stuff of narrative fiction or nonfiction – can become vehicles of healing when they have a particular resonance with our own.

Thirdly, the Father's story – the big story of the Bible – can become the ultimate vehicle of our healing because it is the one book on our planet specifically designed to bring human beings out of the orphanage and into the Father's arms. The Bible is an invitation from another world to come home.

THE SON WHO CAME IN FROM THE COLD

There are many stories in the world about homecoming, but the greatest of them all is told by Jesus in the Gospel of Luke chapter 15.

Jesus is engaged in a heated exchange with 'teachers of the law'. His gripe against them was simple. They were portraying God as remote rather than relational, and in the process denying people the possibility of knowing the one whom he called 'Our Father in heaven.' Furthermore, they were excluding a lot of the most fractured and fallen people in their day from knowing this perfect Father, by setting up an exclusion zone consisting of religious rules and regulations that went way beyond anything that God required. In short, they were misrepresenting who God is; they were turning a loving, welcoming Father into a distant lawmaker.

Jesus' answer to this was not to give a sermon or a lecture but to tell three stories – the first about a lost sheep, the second about a lost coin, the third about a lost son. In all three, the lost are found, and when they are, there is a party. The message is clear: the God of Jesus welcomes everyone home and rejoices when they do with extravagant merrymaking.

In the third of the three stories, Jesus focus on a boy who leaves home and goes to a faraway country with his father's money. He spends his dad's hard-earned cash on excessive living and then finds himself broke. Worse still, there's an economic recession and the only job he can find is one cleaning out a local pigpen – a big comedown for a Jewish lad when you consider that in Judaism pigs are regarded as unclean animals.

After a while, the son comes to his senses. He decides that he will go back home and apologize. He will ask for a job cleaning his dad's stables. After all, his father's employees have a far better standard of living than he does. 'I can pay back all I owe my dad by being one of his stable hands.'

The boy starts his journey home.

Meanwhile, his dad has been watching every day and night for months and years, waiting for his son to return.

One morning, he sees a silhouette of a man on the sandy horizon. The shape becomes gradually more defined in the shimmering haze of the midday sun. The father can see that the man is emaciated. His torn robe is hanging from his shoulder. His feet are bare. His body is bruised. His hair is long, unkempt, matted and dirty. His face is sallow and his eyes are sad.

As the man reaches the edge of the village, the father recognizes him.

'My son!' he whispers.

His heart begins to pound. His eyes are full. Pulling up his robe, he starts to run as fast as his tired old legs will carry him.

When he is only a few strides away, the young man falls to his knees. He looks up into his father's face. He is about to say something but before he can, his father's arms are around him. As the boy tries to speak, the father kisses him. Again and again, he kisses his grubby face and his grimy hair.

Then the father lifts the boy to his feet.

'Fetch the best robe, the family ring and that pair of leather shoes I've been keeping for this day,' he cries.

Three servants go rushing back to the father's house. They return and watch with open mouths as their master drapes the festive robe around the boy's shoulders, puts the glinting signet ring on his finger, and stoops to place the special shoes upon his feet.

When the dad gets up, he starts to dance. His legs are thin and frail but that's never going to stop him. 'Kill the fatted calf,' he sings. 'Kill the fatted calf! My son was lost but now is found! My son was dead but now alive!' All the while, he lifts his arms and hops and skips, ecstatic beyond words.

And so the son, bemused by love, is taken by his father's trembling hand.

He's with his dad again.

His homecoming is complete.

And the party of all parties is about to start.

SMALL STORIES, BIG IDEAS

What a story that is! It is in fact a very Jewish kind of story known in Hebrew as the *mashal* and in English as the *parable*. What is a parable? It is a small story that illustrates a big idea. It is a down-to-earth fiction that communicates a heavenly truth.

In this case, the truth is twofold. The first truth that Jesus wants the teachers of the Law (his audience) to recognize is that God is not some angry, legalistic tyrant. Quite the opposite – he's a compassionate, forgiving, demonstrative, extravagantly lavish Father.

God is like the dad in the story.

He is not remote – he is relational.

He is not angry – he is affectionate.

He is not ferocious – he is forgiving.

He is not miserable – he is merry.

I don't know what image of God you have, but I can almost

guarantee that if you went to boarding school it will not be the one that Jesus was trying to convey in this story. Most of us were exposed to a daily dose of organized and institutionalized religion. Most of us, looking back, were bored to tears by the religion of our school chapel. We sang the hymns and said the prayers on automatic pilot. The God of the chapel was a remote God of rules and rituals. He was distant and our allegiance was one of duty not of joy. He was not the outrageously loving Dad of the story of the prodigal. He was not a home for those away from home. He was the God who was far away.

The second truth that Jesus wanted the teachers of the law to recognize is this: that knowing God is not about servitude but sonship. Think about it for a moment. The teachers of the law had essentially turned their followers into slaves. Their whole lives were based on a lie: 'If I obey all God's rules and observe all his rituals then he'll accept me.' What a lot of nonsense that is! God doesn't want us to be slaves. He wants us to be his sons and daughters. That's why the father in Luke 15 refuses to let his son bargain with him. He will not let his son become a servant or a stable hand. That is slavery. He wants his son back. He wants intimacy.

I don't know what image of Christianity you've had in your life, but I can make an educated guess that if you went to boarding school it was more about religious service than it was about revelling in the fact that you were a son or a daughter of God. This was certainly true in my case for the first eight years of boarding school. I saw Christianity as a religious system that required slavish obedience. But Jesus didn't come to start a religion; he came to start a relationship – a relationship between us and the one he called 'Our Father in heaven'. That is sonship, not slavery.

RELATIONSHIP NOT RELIGION

Jesus was the only religious leader in history who taught that God is a loving, Heavenly Father. Think about it: Jesus was called the Son of God. He went around teaching that he was God's Son, something that caused considerable consternation and controversy to both Jews and Romans alike. Whether we like it or not, Jesus had what we might call a filial consciousness – an unshakeable awareness that he was the Son of his Father in heaven. He related to God intimately and affectionately.

The word 'Father' is rich in meaning. In the original language of Jesus, which was Aramaic, the word is *Abba*. This is a tough word to translate. 'Father' is probably too distant. 'Daddy' is probably too familiar. The right translation is somewhere between the two. Whatever translation you choose – 'Dad', 'Papa', 'Dearest Father' – what can't be missed is the closeness. It was this fact that Jesus was trying to communicate when he described the father in the story of the prodigal. That is some revelation. In fact, it is not just unique in the history of world religions – it is the core message in the teaching of Jesus of Nazareth. As Brennan Manning once said, 'The central revelation of Jesus Christ in the New Testament is that God is our *Abba*, our Daddy.'

If God is our loving, perfect Father, then what does that make us? If we are far away from him then we are orphans. We are separated from our father's love, which is, technically, what an orphan is. In the Hebrew language of the Old Testament, the word translated 'orphan' is *yattam* and it means 'a fatherless one'. Those who don't know God as *Abba*, who only know Christianity as a religion not a relationship, are spiritual orphans. They need to come home to the Father's arms and the Father's house. This can only truly happen when we catch a glimpse of who we are (orphans in need of a father) and who God is (a Father to the fatherless).

THE FATHER OF THE FATHERLESS

One of the most extraordinary meetings of my life occurred ten years ago. I had been working at a Ugandan orphanage for a week and was now sitting on a lawn in the palace grounds of the King of Buganda. King Ronnie was his name and he was sitting in an armchair on the lawn. I was a few metres away under a large white awning that protected us from the blazing sun.

As a boy, King Ronnie (Prince Ronnie as he was then) was in my father's house at boarding school. As his housemaster, my dad looked after him from the ages of 13 to 18. When Ronnie's father was assassinated, my dad had to break the news to him. Later my mother was to report that she had never before seen such dignity in the face of such distress. Ronnie simply bowed his head as he heard the tragic news and accepted his destiny. One day, when the infamous dictator Idi Amin was no longer in power, Ronnie would take the throne and rule as his much-loved father had.

From that moment on, my dad looked after him. He did this with many boys. When parents divorced or died, my dad stepped into the gap, often paying the boys' fees so that they could complete their education. He was known to be the kindest teacher in the school. With Ronnie, this meant taking him to his father's funeral. It also meant looking after him as he navigated A levels, eventually guiding him into his university.

As King Ronnie talked to me, we reminisced.

'He was a father to me,' the king said.

'He was a father to many,' I replied. And so we continued. We had been allocated twenty minutes but spoke for several hours.

Before I left, I turned to him and said, 'You know, my father was a father to the fatherless.'

'He was,' the king agreed.

'When I think of God,' I said, 'I think of him.'

'What do you mean?'

'I mean that God is like my dad. He is a father to the fatherless. That's why Jesus called him Father. That's why we are encouraged to pray from our hearts, 'Our Father in heaven'.

The king looked quizzically at me. I knew this was not his religion. It was a far cry from the animistic faith of those around him but I could see that a window had opened in his soul. That window was my father and the view he now was staring at was the Father of the fatherless – the true and living Father, lover of orphans and defender of widows.

'May I pray for you?' I asked.

He nodded and we stood.

As the awning trembled, I laid my hands upon him. He bowed his head. I prayed a simple prayer, that he would come to know the one to whom my dad had pointed – the perfect Father, the world's best Dad.

When I finished, he opened his eyes. They were full. He took me by the hand and thanked me.

And then we left, returning to the orphans in Luwero, whom the king would visit not long afterwards.

STORY-SHAPED THERAPY

I have an immovable conviction that when the Bible is regarded as the Father's story, it becomes profoundly attractive to every soul. Love is irresistible, especially when the person showing it has paid a great price to offer it to you. In my approach to recovery from boarding school pain, I rely on the Bible because there is healing in its pages.

What, then, is involved in a story-shaped healing process?

There are three keys that are critical if our orphan hearts are to experience freedom from the scars of boarding school. These are keys not steps. Healing – especially divine healing – is never a predictable 'how to' formula. It always respects the individuality and dignity of each unique human being. As such, love – especially the Love of all loves – approaches everyone in different ways, respecting the needs of each person concerned. To the one who misses their attachment to their Dad, God comes to them as Abba Father, with open arms and kindly eyes. To the one who misses their attachment to their Mum, God comes to them as El Shaddai – the one who comforts us as a tender mother does. What I'm about to say can never therefore be used as steps. They are keys. Use them in whatever way, in whatever order, in whatever timeframe, feels comfortable and right to you.

Key 1: Own your story

We all have a choice here: to face the pain or run from it. Owning your story means having the courage to face the music even when you hate the tune. In my case, a broken marriage and divorce were the triggers that compelled me to own my story. My ex-wife and my children had told me that I had been emotionally disengaged as a husband and a father. That devastated me. As soon as I admitted to myself that it was true, I had to understand what it was that had led me to become so detached. This then brought me to a part of my story that I had kept firmly under lock and key: my abandonment at prep school at the age of 8 – a separation from my home and family that led me to remove my emotion chip and cultivate a boarded heart. I had never seen this part of my life in this way before. It was a part of my story I had to face.

Since then I have tried to encourage others who have homesick souls to cultivate a strategy of prevention. Prevention really is preferable to cure. You can avoid catastrophe by owning your story now. Don't let disaster be the springboard for dealing with your pain. Our lives are like cars. Either we can have a regular MOT and in the process discover the faults that could lead to failure, or we can wait till we have a car crash and discover only then that the faults are there. Which would you prefer? Owning your story now, before the crash, or owning it on the far side of fractured lives?

There is an important point to make here about the timeline of our stories. If we are in mid-life, then we are not yet at the end of our story. Since the time of Aristotle, the plot of a story has consisted of three stages: the beginning, middle and end. More recently, people have spoken of 'the story mountain', pointing out how stories have a rising sense of conflict that stems from a problem, and how that problem is resolved leading to a decrease in tension:

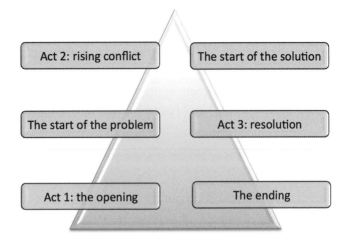

The pain suffered by boarding school orphans occurs during what is the beginning of people's stories. It happens in Act 1. The discovery of the harmful legacy of this abandonment may not occur until Act 2, the middle of our stories. If this is the case for you, then understand this: you can't change the way your story has gone up until now but you can change its trajectory in the future! If you are somewhere towards the end of Act 2, let this epiphany of the pain and its legacy be the inciting incident that propels you into Act 3, and let it be the catalyst for a resolution, not only of the fractures in your soul but the fractures in your relationships too. In short, you write the ending!

Key 2: Tell your story
The next key is to be bold and tell your boarding school story to someone else. For me it was too late to start opening up to my ex-wife in any direct and consistent way about the pain of what I call my 'second orphaning'. My opportunity to tell my

story came when my two oldest and dearest friends invited me every fortnight to their home and set up a counselling session with a first-rate psychotherapist. This person was an expert in the healing of deep-rooted childhood pain. She led me, every fortnight for nearly two years, through a process in which I told my story and she listened, bringing light into my darkness when the need arose.

At first, I was evasive and I used the eloquence I'd learned at boarding school to talk around the issues. Within several sessions she had sussed me out and this was not an option any more. Now I had a choice – either to leave the process or embrace my vulnerabilities. I chose the second.

Whenever anyone opts to share their story, they have to be brave. As writer and speaker Brené Brown says:

> Courage is a heart word. The root of the word courage is *cor* – the Latin word for heart. In one of its earliest forms, the word courage meant 'To speak one's mind by telling all one's heart.' Over time, this definition has changed, and today, we typically associate courage with heroic and brave deeds. But in my opinion, this definition fails to recognize the inner strength and level of commitment required for us to actually speak honestly and openly about who we are and about our experiences – good and bad. Speaking from our hearts is what I think of as 'ordinary courage'.[25]

It is vital in the healing process to share your story with someone you can trust and someone who has empathy as well as understanding. I was very fortunate to have a person like this – a Christian psychotherapist who was both insightful and empathic, and who above all was utterly trustworthy. This issue of trust is critical. Be careful that you only share with someone who loves you and who will never under any conditions divulge your secrets, or with someone who is bound by their profession to a vow of confidentiality. If you can find such people, you will find it far easier to have the courage to narrate your story and in the process receive healing.

Sharing your story is a vital key to our freedom because it brings an end to secrecy. Secrecy is the fertile soil in which the weeds of shame grow and flourish. When you start to narrate your story about boarding school, you have already started the healing process. Shame simply cannot survive when a person begins to share with trusted people about the wounds of abandonment and abuse they suffered when they were very young.

Telling our story is the most effective weedkiller in the world.

It eradicates our shame.

Key 3: Connect your story

One of the best ways to understand your own story is by connecting it within a larger story of the same genre. The genre of a story is simply the kind of story being told. In the world of fiction there are many genres or kinds of story: police procedural dramas, horror stories, whodunits, vampire fiction, historical novels, thrillers, adventure stories and so on. In the case of boarding school pain, healing starts to come when we seek to live by the maxim of the novelist E.M. Forster, 'only connect'. When we see our own story as part of a much broader genre of boarding school stories, we find freedom in the fact that we are not alone. The act of reading other people's stories, albeit imaginary ones, subverts the debilitating power of isolation and creates a sense of community where none existed before.

In the world of fiction, there are many stories that can bring a sense of connection. One example is Roald Dahl's short story called, *Galloping Foxley*, later televised as one of his *Tales of the Unexpected*. Based on a true story, *Galloping Foxley* tells of a man called Perkins who, as a 'contented commuter' one day finds himself sitting opposite a man whom he recognizes as the boy that bullied him at boarding school – a certain Bruce Foxley. Foxley was given the epithet 'galloping' on account of his habit of taking a run up before kicking his victims.

In the short story version, Perkins begins to remember the occasions on which Foxley abused him. These descriptions are of incidents that occurred fifty years previously, and which were so cruel that they later led Perkins to contemplate suicide. Anyone who has been bullied at boarding school – or any kind of school, for that matter – will identify with this poignant storytelling:

I could see myself now, a small pale shrimp of a boy standing just inside the door of this huge room in my pyjamas and bed-room slippers and brown camel-hair dressing-gown. A single bright electric bulb was hanging on a flex from the ceiling, and all around the walls the black and yellow football shirts with their sweaty smell filling the room, and the voice, the clipped, pip-spitting voice was saying, 'So which is it to be this time? Six with the dressing-gown on – or four with it off?'

I never could bring myself to answer this question. I would simply stand there staring down at the dirty floor-planks, dizzy with fear and unable to think of anything except that this other larger boy would soon start smashing away at me with his long, thin, white stick, slowly, scientifically, skilfully, legally, and with apparent relish, and I would bleed. Five hours earlier, I had failed to get the fire to light in his study. I had spent my pocket money on a box of special firelighters and I had held a newspaper across the chimney opening to make a draught and I had knelt down in front of it and blown my guts out into the bottom of the grate; but the coals would not burn.[26]

No wonder Perkins feels as if he's sitting in a cage with a tame tiger.

Stories like this, written by writers who themselves suffered at boarding school, provide moments of connection and can often act as vehicles of healing. This is especially true when we connect our stories with true stories – autobiographical or biographical narratives from those who went through similar experiences to our own and who have managed to find healing and release from decades of pain. Such narrative testimonies are crucial because they work against both isolation and denial. This is one of the main reasons I have included a number of factual testimonies in this book.

HOME AT LAST

Finally, connect your own story with the Big Story of the Father's love – the Bible. As we have seen from the parable of the prodigal son, those of us who have homesick souls can find solace in the homecoming of the prodigal. We can find hope and help in the picture of the father running towards us to embrace us and restore us. Yes, there may be differences between our story and his – not least in the fact that we were sent away from home, whereas the prodigal chose to leave – but the homecoming is what really resonates with us, not the leave taking. Let his story heal your story. The arc of our stories will always be bent towards redemption by the divine storyteller.

Put yourself for a moment in the situation of the prodigal son.

You are far away from home. You have sought every way possible to mask the pain of your inner, wounded child. You have resorted to addictions, using different behaviour patterns and even substances to get through each day. Nothing, however, satisfies.

Now you are in the pigpen. You feel like you have had everything but possessed nothing. You are alone. You are ashamed. You are desperately homesick deep down.

Now, all of a sudden, you begin to reconsider your life. You have a reality check. You miss home. You miss that sense of security and liberty you had in the golden age of your childhood, before boarding school.

You long for a father's embrace and a mother's smile.

You long for your pets and your toys.

You long to be home.

So you turn.

You turn your face towards the One who watches every night and day, aching for your company.

You get up from the mud and mire of all your inner pain – the detritus of damage and disaster.

You start to walk.

You shuffle through the desert of your loneliness until you see him.

Running, weeping, crying out, 'Oh, my daughter!' 'Oh, my son!'

This is your Father – not your earthly dad or mum, but the true Father, your Father in heaven.

As he reaches you, you fall to your knees.

He falls upon your shoulders.

You weep.

He weeps.

'I'm home at last,' you sigh.

And as you do, story starts to bring healing to your broken heart.

7. YESTERDAY'S CHILD

I'll never forget the moment. I was about three months into my fortnightly counselling sessions with my psychotherapist. Up until then we had covered familiar ground as far as my back story was concerned – my birth mother giving my twin sister and me up for adoption, our homecoming to the Stibbe family, the golden years of our childhood between that day and the day we went away to boarding school. Then it dawned on me. Claire and I had been left behind at school just as we'd been left behind at the orphanage. At the age of 8, we had been abandoned. We had been subjected to what I from that moment described as our 'second orphaning'. Unlike our first experience, when we were infants, this time we were painfully aware of it.

When Ebenezer Scrooge began to undergo his dramatic alteration, it was because he was shown how the sadness of his past had contributed to the coldness of his present and the bleakness of his future. In particular, he saw how his abandonment at boarding school had brought such grief into his soul. As a small boy, he had felt solitary and neglected, separated from his father and his sister, fending for himself in the boarding house. Dickens tells us that Scrooge saw this wounded child and sobbed.

What is happening here?

In a single word, it is 'revelation'.

When I saw that I had in effect been subjected to a 'second orphaning' at the age of 8, I began to see my inner wounded child. That 8-year-old boy was still crying. I had ignored him all my life, shut him out – drowned out his sobbing with all my striving and busyness.

Now I heard him. It was unmistakable.

The same occurred to Scrooge. Scrooge came to a moment in his life when he was ready to confront his past. For him it was a matter of life and death. If he had carried on as he was, he would have surely gone to his grave as a miserable and miserly soul, not mourned by anyone. But Scrooge experienced revelation. He had a Christmas Eve awakening in which he saw his past, his present and his future. He saw what he had become and what he would become as well. In the end, his revelation morphed into his transformation. As Dickens memorably put it:

> He became as good a friend, as good a master, and as good a man, as the good old city knew, or any other good old city, town, or borough, in the good old world. Some people laughed to see the alteration in him, but he let them laugh, and little heeded them; for he was wise enough to know that nothing ever happened on this globe, for good, at which some people did not have their fill of laughter in the outset; and knowing that such as these would be blind anyway, he thought it quite as well that they should wrinkle up their eyes in grins, as have the malady in less attractive forms. His own heart laughed: and that was quite enough for him.

Scrooge laughed!

Mourning in the night had given way to joy in the morning.
Scrooge had learned to live and love and laugh again.

This is what we can all experience. We too can experience the joy of Christmas Day within our hearts! The wounded child is healed and the healed child is restored, with great rejoicing.

THE CYCLE OF PAIN

In Part 1, we learned how the cycle of boarding school pain begins with **desertion**. When a boy or a girl is sent away to school, they may believe in their heads that this will be the making of them, but in their hearts they fear that it may be the breaking of them too. For many, the sadness they feel at being sent away from home is indescribable, almost intolerable. While there may be some who see boarding school as a glorious and extended sleepover or the lesser of two evils, for most it feels like exile. We are no longer home; instead, we find ourselves in an orphanage for the privileged.

This then leads to a sense of **deprivation**. Although our circumstances speak of opulence, our hearts come face to face with the awful agony of deprivation. This paradox between external privilege and internal pain is intensified by the growing recognition that our basic needs for love and home cannot be met. The institution cannot parent us. Our housemaster or housemistress cannot be our father or our mother. Matron cannot replace our mum either. No one can. The plea within our hearts for 'Dad' or 'Mum' is never answered here. For months, maybe years, we may cry ourselves to sleep.

How does the wounded child manage this new and harsh reality? The answer is, by living from the mind rather than the heart. The exiled girl or boy begins to disengage themselves emotionally. In response to the loss of attachment, their only survival strategy is **detachment**. Not wanting to be seen as 'wet', they board up their hearts at boarding school. In an attempt to navigate their way through the next ten years, they become mini adults, behaving with the same aloofness as the parents who themselves were sent away to school and who learned to cope by being grown up well before their time.

This strategy of disengagement is, however, fallible. In response to their exile, abandoned children start by intellectualizing their pain but find they need to embrace another strategy too. They anaesthetize as well as intellectualize. They find whatever provides a sense of comfort for them – sport, sex, work, alcohol, playing 'the fool', music, whatever – and they use it to numb the ache within their homesick souls. This, then, is where **dependency** is born and it is the anvil on which an addictive personality is forged. Sometimes these dependencies outlast the years at boarding school and continue into adult life, leaving the ex-boarder dependent on unhealthy attachments that have formed for them a substitute for the often healthy attachments that they knew before they went away to school. In the process, their family and friends become co-dependents – accomplices to their addicted lives.

This, then, is the cycle of pain. So where does the healing begin?

HELP FROM ANOTHER WORLD

A force beyond the purely physical is needed if we are to rescue yesterday's child. This force is love, specifically supernatural love. As Scrooge's story shows, we need engagement with a presence that's more than simply natural if we are to experience the kind of revelation that can take us through to transformation. Dickens called this 'intercourse with the spirits', referring to Scrooge's encounters with the three ghosts of Christmas Past, Present and Future. For us, the encounter is with the three persons of the Trinity – the Father, the Son and the Holy Spirit. When we allow the love of heaven to have access to our hearts, we meet the solitary and neglected child within, just as Scrooge did.

I am one of the first to say that psychotherapy helps enormously and is invaluable in our recovery. We need trusted psychotherapists as they know about deep rooted childhood pain, especially pain associated with the loss of attachment, who will also know about the tendency to disassociate during times of trauma. In addition to a process of wonderful counselling, we need an encounter with the one whom the Bible calls the 'Wonderful Counsellor'. The good news is this: as the prophet Isaiah declared, a child has been born into this world that fits that description perfectly:

> For to us a child is born, to us a son is given, and the government will be on his shoulders. And he will be called Wonderful Counsellor, Mighty God, Everlasting Father, Prince of Peace. Isaiah 9:6

His name is Jesus.

When I embarked on my journey of psychotherapy, I spent every fortnight in the presence of a wonderful Christian counsellor. Her empathy and insight were essential in the healing process. But even she would agree that the breakthrough began to happen when I asked her permission one afternoon to pray.

Bound by certain rules of the counselling profession, she was not allowed to initiate this herself but when I asked, she immediately agreed. We welcomed the presence of God in the room. As soon as that happened, I saw things I had never seen before about myself. More than that, I began to see the Wonderful Counsellor. As I will share in a later chapter, I saw how the *Prince of Shalom* wanted to re-integrate my fractured soul.

THE CYCLE OF HEALING

It was while I was staying in a friend's house in Warwickshire that I had a light bulb moment that led not only to the writing of this book but also the launch of the webinars on the healing of boarding school pain. I woke up early one morning, sometime around 5 a.m., and began reflecting on the transformation brought about by my psychotherapy, particularly as a result of my counsellor recommending that I read Nick Duffell's book *The Making of Them*. This had given me permission to look at an area of my life that I had boarded up since I was 8 years old. It had also given me a framework for understanding what I had been suffering: boarding school pain. I cannot express how grateful I am to Nick for his courageous and pioneering work in this much-neglected area. I can't imagine what it has cost him to stand up for the victims of abandonment and abuse at boarding school.

As I lay in bed, I sensed two things. The first was that I was not just to receive healing – I was to give it away. I had gone through a painful process of dismantling and discovery. I was not to keep what I had learned to myself but share it with the countless number of men and women who are still boarding school orphans.

The second thing I sensed was that there is a cycle of pain and a cycle of healing. The stages of each of these cycles came to me in the form of alliterative words that drifted into my conscious mind. In relation to the cycle of pain, the words were **desertion**, **deprivation**, **detachment** and **dependency**. In relation to the cycle of healing, the words were **revelation**, **restoration**, **reconnection** and **recovery**. These are the positive counterparts and antidotes to the negative phases in the cycle of pain:

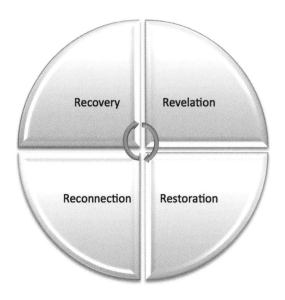

As I continued to ponder these things in my heart, I saw that the healing process begins with **revelation**. If the cycle of pain starts with desertion, then there needs to be a full revelation of that experience and its impact on our lives. Since much of this impact is spiritual not just psychological, this revelation needs to be tantamount to a Scrooge-like awakening. In other words, there has to be a sense in which we see what we haven't seen before, and see that with our spiritual not just our physical eyes. This involves revelation – an unveiling of what has up until now been hidden.

The next phase in the process involves **restoration**. In my view, it may not be possible for us to restore what was lost. Our loved ones may now be dead or they may not be in a position to process what we have discovered. In that event, we need to understand that the pain of abandonment cannot be covered up by simply stating new truths about ourselves. This is putting a plaster on a severe wound. We need more than a cognitive or mindful approach – we need an affective encounter with the Love of all loves.

In my experience, restoration only truly and effectively happens when we displace a negative experience with a positive experience. If the negative experience is the loss of attachment to our parents, then the positive experience we need is the embrace of God, i.e. an attachment to our Father in heaven. When we encounter the Father's love, we come home. As the prodigal discovered, attachment to the Father is the one and only thing that ultimately fills the void left by the loss of earthly attachments.

When this phase of restoration is underway, we begin to release forgiveness to those who have wounded us, especially those who have abandoned or abused us. This extremely challenging task of forgiving others from the heart, and forgiving ourselves as well, leads to the third phase of **reconnection**, in which the thinking and feeling parts of the soul get reunited and we start to cultivate what Dan Goleman calls 'emotional intelligence' – the ability to understand, manage and express our feelings in a healthy way.[27] It is in this phase that we start to reconnect those parts of us that became stuck at a very young age while we were going through our boarding school pain. These parts need to be owned and reintegrated – a process that in my experience requires an encounter with the Wonderful Counsellor.

When all this is in process, we can now engage in the fourth phase of our healing which is **recovery** – that is to say, freedom from all the dependencies we have developed in order to anaesthetize our pain. Once the Love of all loves satisfies the father and mother hunger in our lives, we no longer have any need of substances, behaviours, relationships, technologies or ideologies to numb our aching hearts. Recovery means displacing unhealthy attachments with the healthiest attachment in the universe – the attachment of our hearts to the Father's love. Nothing can compare with that.

EMBRACING VULNERABILITY

The first step in the healing process is therefore revelation, and this primarily involves an honest recognition of what was done to us when we were sent away to school and the legacy of these experiences.

Yes, I said 'honest'.

Early on in my counselling journey, my psychotherapist listened while I spoke. I can't remember what I was saying but I had been going on a long time and I was using words to cover up my vulnerability.

'Can I stop you there,' she said.

'Er, okay,' I stammered.

'Who am I listening to?' she asked.

'What do you mean?'

'I mean, am I listening to "slick Mark" or "real Mark"?'

That was a game-changing moment. I realized I was in the presence of someone who could see right through the 'gift of the gab' learned at boarding school. From that time on, I told the truth. I bared my soul.

At one point during the following weeks, I started opening up about my boarding school years. I don't remember how we got onto the subject. All I do know is that I had kept this part of my life buried. I had been extremely honest about my experience of being abandoned by my birth mother as a baby but I had never really talked to anyone about the day I was left by my adoptive parents on the front drive of my prep school.

'What do you remember?' she asked.

Immediately I was in touch with yesterday's child. I cannot say for sure how much of what I remembered had been suppressed but the moment she gave me permission to talk, I began to relive the moment.

And the feelings came flooding back with it.

Before I left, my counsellor set me a challenge. 'I want you to try and write down a conversation about what you've just shared – a conversation between today's Mark and your 8-year-old Mark.'

'Er, okay!'

'I want you to let your 8-year-old Mark speak.'

'That feels a bit weird.'

'Just give it a try. Oh . . . and one more thing . . .'

'Yes?'

'Is there somewhere safe you can go to in your house if you

start to find this difficult?'

I was living on my own in Wantage at that time, in my mother's house. She was by then in a nursing home in Suffolk, so the place was unoccupied. In a conservatory full of books and flowers, there was a safe place for me – an armchair in the corner, underneath a standard lamp.

It was where my beloved father sat in the last years of his life.

'I'll use my father's chair,' I said.

MY FATHER'S CHAIR

When I next saw my counsellor, I read what I had written. In what you're about to read, TM stands for Today's Mark. YM stands for Yesterday's Mark.

TM: I want to welcome you Mark. You're in a safe place. Please share what happened on your eighth birthday.

YM: I was sent away.

TM: How did that make you feel?

YM: I felt sad and lonely. I wanted my parents to turn the car around, come back and take me home.

TM: Can you say a bit more?

YM: I was left behind and alone, with nothing but my trunk and my teddy bear, in a strange place I'd never been before; left in the care of a man I didn't trust.

TM: It's totally okay to be angry and sad about this.

YM: It doesn't feel right to be angry or sad.

TM: Why not?

YM: It feels ungrateful.

TM: Why do you think that?

YM: Because my mother always used to say that people had sacrificed a lot for me to be there. So I feel like I'm being ungrateful to my parents for saying that it was painful.

TM: It's perfectly okay to feel that way and it's even more okay to say it. For whatever reason, you were abandoned by your parents that day and for the next ten years of your life. Do you think you can forgive them?

YM: I love them.

TM: But can you forgive them?

YM: Yes, I can. I do forgive them.

TM: Was that the worst feeling you experienced that day?

YM: No.

TM: Can you say what else affected you?

YM: The headmaster. When my parents left, he took me inside.

TM: Did he hurt you?

YM: I just knew he was scary. As soon as my parents had driven off, he was different with me from the way he had been with them.

TM: What did you sense?

YM: I could see from his eyes that he was a very cruel man and I felt really scared.

TM: Tell me more about that.

YM: He beat me . . . six of the best with a bamboo cane . . . on my first night, in front of the whole dormitory. The pain was unbearable. I felt so ashamed for crying. I was bleeding.

TM: It's all right to feel that. You were a victim. You had done nothing to deserve it.

YM: I wanted to sob but I could tell that if I did, the others in the dorm would call me 'wet'.

TM: So how did you deal with that?

YM: I hugged my bear under my bed sheets after lights out and cried quietly into his shoulder.

TM: What went through your mind?

YM: That somehow my bear and I would get through all of this. But to do that there had to be no more crying, no more weakness. It was time to grow up and survive.

TM: So you grew up at 8 years old?

YM: Yes.

TM: Don't you think you missed years of happy childhood because of that?

YM: At least five years, yes.

TM: Mark, this was abandonment and abuse. Your abandonment by your parents was not meant that way but it had that effect. Your abuse, on the other hand, was intentional. It was cruel and terrifying. You were wronged.

YM: I *was* wronged.

TM: Can you forgive that headmaster?

YM: I guess I have to.

TM: Then try to forgive him.

YM: I forgive you, headmaster.

TM: How do you feel?

YM: Better, lighter, freer.

TM: Mark I want you to come to Jesus now. You didn't know Jesus back then. But I know him. He's the kindest, safest man in the universe. He wants you to walk to him. He's going to hug you and when he does, the pain is going to go away.

YM: How?

TM: He'll show you that you've never really been alone, never will be.

YM: But what about the abuse?

TM: He's going to show you that he experienced abuse on the cross and his wounds are going to heal your wounds.

YM: I don't understand.

TM: You don't have to. All you have to do is walk to him now. He'll do the rest.

YM: Will I be free?

TM: Yes.

YM: I want that so much.

TM: Then come to Jesus. He'll take care of it all. He's really good at this. There's nobody better.

Waiting for My Dad

I know, from personal experience, how hard it is to let someone into these secret places of shame. Many of us are like old and spacious houses. We have locked away our most painful memories in a trunk and hidden them in a dusty corner of the attic of our lives. There they stay until the day arrives when the light begins to shine in the darkness. When we trust enough to let this light into the secret places of our hearts, we open up the trunk and let the Healer in. One by one, he takes each memory out – a teddy, a cricket bat, an exercise book, a handkerchief. One by one, he shines his light on each, and as our tears begin to flow he heals the shame. Then, when all the memories are done, he opens up the windows in the loft. The sun pours in and all the sadness in the hidden, hurting heart is dissipated.

There is no healing in concealing, only in revealing. We have to learn to trust enough to share our story.

Not long ago my wife and I received this poignant testimony from a woman called Lucy:

My brother and I were born in the eighties and we lived in a very affluent part of Accra, Ghana in West Africa. We lived in a big house with our older siblings from my dad's previous marriages, my grandma, house helps and dogs. My parents separated when I was very young.

The next I remember, my dad was moving back to England and we were put in the back of my dad's Volvo, as we were many times during trips to the beach at weekends. Only this time my brother and I were taken to a relative we hardly knew, who was to look after us.

We lived with her and her family for a few years until the day our granddad turned up, claiming he was taking us to live with our dad. We were so happy to see him. To hear that we were going to live with Dad again was exciting too; we were being mistreated by our relatives.

Instead of going to my father's house, however, we were surprised to arrive at a boarding school in the middle of nowhere. Most of the boarding schools those days were situated outside towns. This one was next to a firing range. It was a mixed school for both boys and girls from the ages of 6 to 14.

My granddad pulled into the car park and told us he was visiting a friend. We walked up to the headmaster's house and they spoke a few words to each other. Before we knew it, my granddad said that he was leaving. I remember standing at the balcony of the headmaster's two-storey house, from which I could see almost the whole compound, including the dormitories, the dining hall of the school and also the main road leading to the school. I broke down in tears and pleaded with my granddad not to leave me there. He assured me my dad would come and pick me up soon.

I waited and waited for my dad to come and pick me up, but he never turned up.

In the end, I gave in and went along with my house assistant who comforted me and took me to my dormitory, showed me my bed and walked me around the compound.

The next day I went back to the balcony of the headmaster's house again where I could have a better view of the main road leading to the school.

I was hoping to see my dad.

I did that for a week or so, and finally gave up.

I was only 6 years old at this point and this was the beginning of my boarding school experience. I felt abandoned, rejected, unwanted, unloved, helpless and hopeless.

In Ghana at the time, most parents were living abroad so they depended on external family members to care for their children during vacation times. When term finished and other children were being picked up, my brother and I would find ourselves wondering who would be picking us up. It was a different family member every time. They were all paid by our dad to look after us. We did not have a home or parents to go home to. During half-terms we stayed on campus with a few other kids who, like us, did not have homes to go to.

We lived like this for years until, when I was 12, our mum picked us up and took us to live with her in Accra, Ghana.

At the age of 18, I moved to England to further my education.

It took extraordinary courage for Lucy to open up to us about her inner pain, but in describing her abandonment by her father she embraced vulnerability and began to experience healing from the perfect Father, the one who promises never to leave or forsake us.

Sooner or later, we all need to do the same.

We need to climb into the loft and open up the trunk.

We need to share our stories.

We need to introduce yesterday's child to the Father we've been waiting for all our lives.

NAMING THE WOUND

If we are to receive healing, we must dare to share our story. We need to articulate the fact that when we were sent away to school we no longer enjoyed daily access to our parents. We were ripped from their arms and placed in a strange place, often far from home. Consequently, from that time on, we lost our attachment to our parents and a seed of shame was planted in our souls. This shame was often worsened by the beatings and the bullying we faced, all of which increased our insecurity and reinforced the sense that somehow we were never good enough. To cope with this, we became performance oriented, always trying to earn approval through achievement. We became addicted to whatever comforted us and masked our homesickness.

Put like that, we are left with only one conclusion: *what I'm describing here is an orphan*. We may have been in a country house or a stately home, but the place where we were left became for us an orphanage. Sooner or later, we all have to come to recognize that even though we may have had a mum or dad when we were sent away to boarding school, we effectively became orphans the day they drove away.

This is what we are – boarding school orphans.

If orphans are people separated from their father and their mother's love, then this is what we are.

If orphans are people who feel a sense of shame at being left behind and left alone, then this is what we are.

If orphans are people who are driven to earn affirmation through performance, then this is what we are.

If orphans are people who live on the surface level and hide their true emotions, then this is what we are.

If orphans are people who are afraid of being separated again from those they love, then this is what we are.

If orphans are people who build a false sense of identity in order to survive, then this is what we are.

If orphans are people who seek to mask their inner pain through addictive behaviours, then this is what we are.

If orphans are people who find it hard to engage in intimate and lifelong relationships, then this is what we are.

If orphans are people who search for substitute fathers and mothers, often in unhealthy relationships, then this is what we are.

If orphans are people who feel alone and have no one they can really share their heart with, then this is what we are.

If orphans are people who wonder whether there is really any hope or future, then this is what we are.

If orphans are people who hoard money and possessions through a fear of lack, then this is what we are.

If orphans are people who have a cloud of sadness perpetually hovering over their hearts, then this is what we are.

Sooner or later, the true wound has to be revealed.

Yesterday's child has to be healed.

AN END TO DENIAL

There are three sorts of reaction we need to guard against if yesterday's child is to experience healing.

The first is the response that says, 'I'm not aware I have a problem.' I meet ex-boarders who often say this. Sometimes this is because the person simply cannot remember anything about their boarding school days. They have buried their negative memories of boarding school and repressed their feelings in the process. If a person is to receive healing, they have to dare to share their story. As they do, they will start to remember, and in the act of remembering, they will come face to face with their wound.

The second is the response that says, 'My experience wasn't that bad.' What we need to remember here is that everyone's experience of boarding school is different. Some people endure extreme abuse in addition to abandonment. Their experience is an update of *Tom Brown's Schooldays*. At the same time, all of us share something in common. If we were sent away to school, we were separated from our parents' love. Our primal attachments were ruptured. That means we are all orphans, whether we were abused or not.

The third is the response that says, 'I didn't suffer at all.' This reaction may be genuine in some people. Some, without doubt, had positive experiences at boarding school. They enjoyed the friends they made and the opportunities they received. I did too. At the same time, there is a boarding school stoicism that covers up the real facts and the real facts were simply this: that we were separated from our parents' love and there were harmful consequences. No amount of stiff-upper-lip bravado can disguise this.

What we need to be aware of here is that ex-boarders don't just intellectualize or anaesthetize their pain – they minimize it too. This is denial and denial is the territory of the orphan. As I showed in my book *I Am your Father*, the reflex of the orphan heart is to conceal our true feelings and to be selective in remembering the past.[28] Orphans opt for fantasy rather than reality, building a version of their lives that enables them to continue to survive. In doing this, they are bound, not free.

Most people, when they hear me tell my story, or read what I have written, begin to see that all is far from well within their hearts. Even when they have submitted to a process of counselling and prayer in other Christian contexts, they find that the specific issues relating to boarding school pain remain buried. As one elderly man wrote to me, shortly after listening to a webinar I gave on this subject:

> I have now listened to the introductory recording and I am sure that this is a very timely course for me. I thought I had worked through all the boarding school stuff in my life but listening to the recording I found the Lord speaking into my life and, on occasions, the tears witnessed to that! I pray that after this course I will not only have 'come home' but that others will also be set free in Jesus' name.'

Isn't it time for all of us to come home?

Homecoming begins when we choose to let go of denial as a coping mechanism and we start instead to own, share and connect our story.

We acknowledge that we are orphans and in the process

remove the boards that have covered our broken hearts.

We start to let others into the hidden, hurting places of our hearts, revealing who and what we really are to trusted others in our world.

As soon as we commit ourselves to this courageous process, the tears begin to flow, and so does the healing.

8. RESTORING THE YEARS

During recent times, I have had a number of people say to me, 'The Lord is going to restore the years that the locusts have eaten.' This promise has always brought immense comfort. After having lost so much as a direct result of not dealing with my boarding school pain, not to mention my own poor choices, this is such a reassuring word of hope. Yes there may be a sense that 'what's lost is lost', as one member of my family – an atheist – once said, but when we submit our stories to the divine storyteller, it is amazing how he can bring redemption to even the most desperate situations. He can turn our mistakes into miracles.

So what does it mean to have a restoration of the years that the locusts have eaten? This promise, taken from Joel 2:25, needs to be set in context. The first chapter of the book of Joel describes the devastating consequences of an invasion of locusts in the land of Israel:

> What the chewing locust left, the swarming locust has eaten;
> What the swarming locust left, the crawling locust has eaten;
> And what the crawling locust left, the consuming locust has eaten.
> Joel 1:4, NKJV

The prophet describes the effects on Israel's crops:

The vine has dried up,
And the fig tree has withered;
The pomegranate tree,
The palm tree also,
And the apple tree—
All the trees of the field are withered;
Surely joy has withered away from the sons of men.
Joel 1:12, NKJV

Faced with this dreadful plight, the prophet urges his hearers to turn back to the Lord with all of their heart. God is full of grace and mercy, slow to anger and full of kindness. When we return to this loving Father, he will restore us. This is his promise, as the prophet declares:

I will restore to you the years that the swarming locust has eaten,
The crawling locust,
The consuming locust,
And the chewing locust,
My great army which I sent among you.
You shall eat in plenty and be satisfied,
And praise the name of the LORD your God,
Who has dealt wondrously with you;
And My people shall never be put to shame.
Joel 2:25–26, NKJV

Restoration is on the way and this restoration is not just physical, affecting the natural world, but spiritual, bringing refreshment to the soul:

> And it shall come to pass afterward
> That I will pour out My Spirit on all flesh;
> Your sons and your daughters shall prophesy,
> Your old men shall dream dreams,
> Your young men shall see visions.
> And also on My menservants and on My maidservants
> I will pour out My Spirit in those days.
> Joel 2:28–29, NKJV

THE LOST YEARS

As I wrote in Chapter 3, the boarding school experience presents a child with a startling paradox: 'the painful privilege'. *Externally* the surroundings could not appear more abundant, nor the opportunities. *Internally* the landscape looks very different – bleak and barren, bereft of all the things that bring a sense of wellbeing and happiness in the child's heart. The word that describes this inner map is 'deprivation'. As I showed in Chapter 3, the child often feels deprived of seven bare necessities of life:

1. Love

No matter how hard the boarding school tries, it can never compensate for the loss of the love of a father and a mother in a boarder's life. The institution cannot become a surrogate parent and nor can the staff who work in it. The child is quite simply abandoned in an orphanage for the privileged.

2. Home

However impressive the school buildings are – and many give the impression of giving a boarder a decade in Hogwarts – the boarding school can never compensate for the loss of home, especially if 'home' has been a happy, secure and familiar reality to the child.

3. Safety

While boarding schools take great care to watch over their children, they can never monitor the safety of a child in the way that parents do when their children are growing up in the home. Abuse happens at all sorts of different levels. Boarding schools can at times feel very unsafe indeed.

4. Childhood

As I showed in Chapter 3, the boarder often makes a choice to survive the years of exile at boarding school by behaving like a mini adult. This means emulating the emotionally detached behaviour of parents (many of whom were also sent away to school) and in turn leads to the loss of childhood.

5. Siblings

While some boarders are fortunate to have their siblings at the same boarding school, for many of them, being sent away means separation, not only from parents, pets and toys but from brothers and sisters. If these relationships have been healthy, no new friendships can make up for this loss.

6. Innocence

Many boarders lose their sexual innocence while away at school. Sometimes these first sexual encounters are abusive. While such toxic experiences can be shared by non-boarders, boarders do not have the parental oversight and guidance they need at such critical moments.

7. Freedom

The boarder's life is a strictly regimented existence. At least for non-boarders there is the prospect of time after school, and at the weekends, where they are free. Not so with boarders, for whom every hour is filled with tasks that serve an intensely performance-oriented social system.

What happens to boys and girls who are deprived of these basic needs? The consequences can be very destructive. The soul of the boarder becomes homesick. The heart becomes boarded.

To use the language of Joel, the locusts devour the abundance in the landscape of the boarder's soul.

The child feels as if he or she has been put to shame.

Joy withers away from the sons and daughters of men.

TAKING RESPONSIBILITY

How can such a life be restored? Is it possible to have love, home, safety, childhood, siblings, innocence and freedom restored? Or is this simply a fairy tale, the stuff of make believe?

It is here that we need to focus on our own story rather than fixing our attention on the stories of those whom we have loved. I cannot emphasize this more strongly. Our first responsibility is not to change the situations that these locusts have produced, including all the impaired and broken relationships. It may or may not be possible for these to be transformed. Our responsibility is to focus on what we can change and that is our own hearts. In other words, we need to take ownership for our own soul care, praying the simple prayer, 'Change me', rather than, 'Change them'.

This is a principle I have come not only to understand but also to embrace. I cannot change my father or my mother. My dad is dead and my mother is, at this very moment, very close to the end. I cannot make it my responsibility to change their thinking about boarding school, or to change their feelings about it and what it reproduced in my life. My task is to focus on my own heart and to identify what was lost when I went away to school. My mission is to own my story and to share my story, and in doing so to end the secrecy and shame and to open myself up to the possibility of transformation.

Taking hold of your responsibility is the first step in your restoration. You cannot activate your dependence on institutions at this point. Many ex-boarders move from one institution to another. They start as children at boarding school and then they go on to study at university, and join professions in institutions such as the army or the Church. Some even go back to boarding school as teachers. Many never know anything other than institutional life. The institution provides what they need, standing in effect *in loco parentis*. In relation to our healing, however, we cannot look to the institution to do this. What we need, it cannot provide.

The reason why taking responsibility is so important is because one of the characteristics of the orphan is entitlement. The orphan doesn't take responsibility for their own healing because the orphan regards it as the responsibility of the state or the institution to give them what they need. Whenever a person decides to change this default setting, they begin to take their first tentative steps towards freedom. They recognize that they have homesick souls and boarded hearts and they do whatever is necessary to become whole and an instrument of healing to others.

The ideal of wholeness is, ironically, one of the core values that undergird the boarding school system itself. My father, who spent twenty-seven years teaching in a British public school, used to quote the Roman poet Juvenal, saying that the purpose of a boarding school education was to produce healthy minds in healthy bodies (*mens sana in corpora sano*).[29] In other words, it was to develop young men and women who were 'rounded', to use the traditional word. Today I believe this: that to be whole or rounded does indeed mean having a healthy mind but having a healthy mind ironically means dealing with the pain inflicted by the boarding school system.

It is therefore critical to take responsibility for your own transformation. Don't at this stage try and transform impaired relationships with your parents, teachers, siblings, spouse, children or whoever. Where healing is still possible in these relationships, it will come as a result of you seeking inner change for yourself, not from you seeking to change them. When you change, they will change. This is the divine order. Any attempt to change them first is control, control is born of fear, and fear is born of shame. In other words, the 'change them' mentality is an orphan mindset. It is not conducive to having a healthy mind in a healthy body.

FROM SURVIVING TO THRIVING

It is now acknowledged that getting ex-boarders to tell their story and face the pain is one of the toughest challenges in psychotherapy. Why is this? It is, first and foremost, because ex-boarders learned at an early age how to bury their feelings, even to dissociate from them. It should therefore come as no surprise that ex-boarders who undergo psychotherapy often pull out of the process just at the moment when the light comes on and they see clearly what their abandonment and sometimes also abuse did to them. Getting an ex-boarder to admit their need for psychotherapeutic help is tough enough. Getting them to stay the course and work their way through the pain until the breakthrough has come is an even tougher ask.

One way to resolve this problem is through imaginative incentivization. In other words, ex-boarders need to catch a glimpse of what life might look like on the far side of the process. What kind of life does the ex-boarder live right now? Nick Duffell provides a list of some of the words that are uttered by attendees at his boarding school survivors' workshops.[30]

- Neglect
- Betrayal
- Abandonment
- Grief
- Rage
- Abuse
- Confusion
- Sadness
- Helplessness

- Loneliness
- Motherless
- Missing Daddy
- Sent away
- Neediness
- Suppression
- Denial
- Tears
- Survival

Are these words that you would use about your own life?

In my book *I Am Your Father: What Every Heart Needs to Know*, I provided a list of the signs and symptoms – the external and internal traits – of the orphan heart condition.[31] The words you've just read align with many of the signs and symptoms of the orphan's experience. Not dealing with your boarding school pain therefore has serious consequences. In effect, it turns you into a boarding school orphan. Remaining an orphan means surviving and existing. It does not mean thriving and really living.

This is why ex-boarders need to be incentivized. We need a picture of what life might look like the far side of the therapeutic process. We need to dream a little. We need to focus on ourselves as the transformed Scrooge, not the unredeemed Scrooge. This means letting our imaginations dream about rediscovering our lost inner child and releasing that child to celebrate Christmas Day every day. It means imagining what life would be like when we no longer feel abandoned, lonely, betrayed, neglected or sad – when we no longer miss Daddy and no longer feel motherless.

Taking responsibility for dealing with boarding school

pain might therefore become a less arduous challenge if we incentivized ourselves and others with a picture of what it might look like to experience a restoration of all those years the locusts have eaten.

What does it look like to be awakened?

What does it look like to be transformed?

What does it look like to be free?

What does it look like to be really alive?

FIRST THE BAD NEWS

In order to experience the full benefits of the restoration phase in the cycle of healing we need first of all to look again at what was lost when we were sent away to boarding school. What most of us were robbed of can be summed up in one simple phrase: 'healthy attachments'.

The notion of 'attachment' is critical in receiving healing from boarding school pain and here the work of John Bowlby and others is significant and insightful.[32] Bowlby argued that healthy attachments to our parents in childhood are critical if we are to live fully satisfying lives in adulthood. Those whose attachments are positive as children grow up with a strong sense of self-worth, security and significance. They are able to love and to receive love. They believe that the world is a safe place and they engage in relationships with others that are rich and rewarding. The dependency relationship which we have with our mothers and fathers is therefore essential for our emotional health, not just in childhood but in later life too. When the attachment is strong, particularly between the infant and their mother in the earliest years, the goodness of this unbroken intimacy can last a lifetime.

The problem is that not everyone enjoys a childhood in which their attachment to Mum and Dad is protected and nurtured. Those whose attachments to their parents are ruptured experience damaging consequences. They become 'attachment disordered' children and the negative legacy of this can last a lifetime too. Their development as children is impaired. Their perception of relatedness with others is damaged. They grow up with a defective concept of who they are and their life experiences – especially their relationships with others – are severely impoverished.

If you have been sent away to boarding school, you experienced a most unnatural rupture in your attachment to your mother and father. This separation did not typically come about through any natural process, such as death, but through the choice your parents made to send you away to an institution where attachment deprivation was the common denominator. This caused you to grow up far too quickly because you chose to become a mini adult as a survival mechanism. This then resulted in shut down emotions and set you up for a life of detachment in which you have found it almost impossible to engage with your spouse, partner, children or others at an emotionally healthy level. It set in motion a tendency to depend on unhealthy attachments as a compensation for the healthy attachments that you lost. All this means that even in your later years, deep down you are still that traumatized child abandoned at the entrance to a country house; deep down you are still yearning for your mother and your father; deep down you long for yesterday's child to come on home.

Now the Good News
One of my convictions about 'attachment theory' is that it is

stronger on diagnosis than it is on prognosis. How is such attachment disorder to be healed? How are ex-boarders really to be set free from the awful consequences of ruptured and impaired attachments? Is it enough for me to look at the list of positive beliefs about myself, and others, and simply recite them every day and night as I look at myself in the mirror? Is a purely cognitive approach, based on positive thinking, enough to restore the years that the locusts have eaten? Is acknowledging and telling my story enough? Is a purely psychotherapeutic approach going to set me free?

The answer is, not completely. Attachment theory is helpful when it comes to identifying the trauma of being sent away to school, not to mention the consequences of that wound, but it is inadequate in its present form to heal the wounds of abandonment and to bring about the kind of internal restoration that leads to external transformation. For this to happen we are really talking about something more than a purely psychotherapeutic approach. We are talking about a spiritual perspective that enables us to receive deep and lasting healing for the wounds that still afflict the soul. As the story of Scrooge constantly and insistently reminds us, we need something akin to a supernatural intervention to turn our hearts of stone into hearts of flesh.

It is here that all my previous work on the orphan heart condition and its healing has become so important, not only to my own recovery but to the recovery of many other ex-boarders too. For over twenty years I have stressed the same point in books like *I Am Your Father* – that true healing for broken attachments is found in the Father's embrace. I have argued consistently that it is not enough for a person whose inner child feels 'motherless' and says, 'I miss Daddy' to simply acknowledge that wound. It is not enough for them to try and resolve their negative experience by adopting and reciting positive beliefs. The only way to deal with a negative experience is by displacing it with a positive experience.

What does this mean in practice?

It means going back to the revelation that we explored in the previous chapter – the revelation encapsulated in the soul-stirring words from Psalm 27: 'Even if my father and my mother abandon me, the Lord will hold me close' (Ps. 27:10, NLT).

It is in the Father's arms that we find true healing.

When he holds us close, he hugs the hell out of us, just as the prodigal son discovered.

OUR HEALTHIEST ATTACHMENT

Lasting healing from broken attachments comes when we resort not to toxic attachments to substances, people, ideologies and behaviours but when we come to a place where we cry out to God, 'I feel motherless, but your mother-like embrace is my comfort. I miss my earthly daddy, but in your arms I know that you're the perfect Dad, the one who will never leave nor forsake me.' When we eventually stop trying to control everything in our lives – as Scrooge tried – and surrender ourselves to an intervention from heaven, then the healing begins. As we present our boarding school pain to the Father, and enter into a spiritual attachment to him, it is then that we begin to experience the restoration of all those years that the locusts have eaten. Our withered souls begin to rejoice and the landscape of our hearts turns from barrenness to blessing. We find that the long, hard, winter of frozen feelings is at an end and the season of singing has come at last.

In other words, a cognitive approach is not enough. We need an affective encounter as well!

The answer to the deprivations I described in Chapter 3 is therefore restoration, and restoration comes first through acknowledging the simple truth that we became orphans when our attachment to our parents was ruptured at an early age. Secondly, it comes through opening up our souls to the healthiest attachment of all – to the one who created us right from the beginning for attachment to him, our Father in heaven. When we feel his divine embrace, then our orphan hearts are healed.

Experiencing the Love of all loves is therefore, in my experience, a prerequisite in the psychotherapeutic process. No counterfeit versions of this divine attachment can in any way displace the wounds of abandonment and abuse. No cognitive therapy in which I declare positive beliefs in an attempt to remove the effects of a negative experience will ultimately set me free. I have to do what Scrooge did: acknowledge the pain caused by my experience of abandonment, express remorse for all the poor choices I've made in my attempt to survive, and open my heart to the only love on earth and in heaven that can fill the father and mother-shaped void.

How, then, do I experience this attachment to my Father in heaven?

Let me encourage you to use a story-shaped approach.

Is there a story you know that describes a father's embrace in a way that has deeply moved you?

Can you use this as a parable of the Father's love?

OH! MY DADDY, MY DADDY!

There is a particular story that has moved me since the day I first saw it in its celebrated cinematic version. I'm referring to E. Nesbit's *The Railway Children*, a tale about three siblings – Bobbie, Peter and Phyllis – who are separated from their father when he is unjustly accused of selling state secrets to the Russians while working for the Foreign Office. He is taken away from his wife and children for questioning. The mother and three children, now financially challenged, leave London for a house called The Three Chimneys in Yorkshire. It stands near a railway line, on which they have many adventures as they long for their father to return.

There are many features that make this story a timeless classic, but perhaps one big reason for its resonance when I saw it aged 10, and its enduring appeal today, is its theme of the absent father. So many children are growing up now without a dad, as many of my books have discussed and demonstrated. What *The Railway Children* provides is an extraordinarily poignant story of hope that one day that absent dad will return through the mists of time to embrace us – just as he does for his waiting, aching daughter Bobbie in the standout and climactic scene in the movie.

I saw Lionel Jeffries's much-loved film version as a child when my father and mother took me to see it at the Noverre Cinema in Norwich.[33] By that time I had been at prep school for two years and knew a thing or two about absent fathers. I had never known my biological dad at all, and it's clear from recent discoveries that he doesn't even know of my sister's existence or mine. Furthermore, being sent away to boarding school had provided an equally painful experience of broken attachment to a father, this time to my kind and generous adoptive father, Philip Stibbe. So when the train pulled in and the father appeared, the tears began to flow, and still do.

I don't think there are many boarding school orphans that cannot relate to the agonized look on Bobbie's face as she stands at the railway station and watches as the passengers disembark the train on which she hopes beyond hope her father has been travelling.

There are few of us who went away to boarding school who cannot fail to be moved by the sight of the father appearing after everyone else has left the train, walking through the steam.

And then that scream – Bobbie's cry – 'Oh! my Daddy, my Daddy!'

In Nesbit's original story, this scene is described with touching elegance and a telling restraint.

Bobbie was left standing alone, the Station Cat watching her from under the bench with friendly golden eyes.

Of course you know already exactly what was going to happen. Bobbie was not so clever. She had the vague, confused, expectant feeling that comes to one's heart in dreams. What her heart expected I can't tell — perhaps the very thing that you and I know was going to happen — but her mind expected nothing; it was almost blank, and felt nothing but tiredness and stupidness and an empty feeling, like your body has when you have been a long walk and it is very far indeed past your proper dinner-time.

Only three people got out of the 11.54. The first was a countryman with two baskety boxes full of live chickens who stuck their russet heads out anxiously through the wicker bars; the second was Miss

Peckitt, the grocer's wife's cousin, with a tin box and three brown-paper parcels; and the third —

'Oh! my Daddy, my Daddy!' That scream went like a knife into the heart of everyone in the train, and people put their heads out of the windows to see a tall pale man with lips set in a thin close line, and a little girl clinging to him with arms and legs, while his arms went tightly round her.[34]

What a story that is!

Maybe make it your parable of the Father's love.

Ask for a personal revelation of the Father.

WHEN THE HEALING STARTS

Ted Dekker is an American novelist, born in 1962. He has written more than twenty suspense thrillers and is a *New York Times* bestselling author. In 2015 he wrote a novel about the life of Jesus, entitled *A.D. 33*. Before starting the story, Dekker wrote an introduction describing his own religious background. He began by sharing some positive memories about his parents:

I grew up as the son of missionaries who left everything in the West to take the good news to a tribe of cannibals in Indonesia. My parents were heroes in all respects and taught me many wonderful things, not least among them all the virtues and values of the Christian life. What a beautiful example they showed me.[35]

Then the note changes dramatically.

When I was six years old, they did what all missionary parents did in that day and for which I offer them no blame: they sent me to a boarding school. There I found myself completely untethered and utterly alone. I wept that first night, terrified. I don't remember the other nights because I have somehow blocked those painful memories, but my friends tell me that I cried myself to sleep many months.

Dekker now turns to the emotional consequences.

I felt abandoned. And I was only six. I was lost, like that small bird in that children's book who wanders from creature to creature in the forest, asking each if she is his mother.

Are you my mother? Are you my father?

I see now that my entire life since has been one long search for my identity and for significance.

In the subsequent years, throughout his teens in particular, Dekker lived with a feeling of never measuring up. However, Dekker also shares that he eventually found peace not through the religious system of Christianity but through encountering the one in whose own day was known as *Yeshua*, Jesus. This happened as he chose to leave the world of suspense thrillers for a moment and write a novel about the real Jesus – something he had longed to do for ten years. When that happened he came to see how his vision of what Christianity is really all about was blocked by the secret judgements and grievances he had harboured against himself and the world. When he did that, he unlearned all that he had learned and started without prejudice. As a result, he began to know personally the one whom Jesus came to reveal – the Father. As he writes in his introduction, our salvation is found in surrendering what we think we know *about* the Father so that we can truly *know* him, which is to experience him intimately, because this is living eternal life now. It is the great reversal of all that we think will give us significance and meaning in this life so that we can live with more peace and power than we have yet imagined.

In encountering Yeshua and his Father, Dekker believes that 'we will not be bitten by the lie of snakes' and 'we will heal the sickness that has twisted our minds'. This is what Dekker calls 'the Way of Yeshua'. Walking in this Way, we become 'free from the prisons that hold us captive'. As he puts it, 'This is our healing: to see what few see' – the real Jesus, the Peace-Bringer, the One who leads us to the Father.

ROGER'S STORY

More and more ex-boarders are finding healing in the true Father's embrace. One of many examples comes from an attendee on one of our webinar courses on boarding school pain and its healing. In the first session I gave a talk entitled 'Opening an Old Trunk'. Roger wrote to me a few days after this session:

I've not been able to get that image of the trunk and tuck box out of my mind since it flashed up on my laptop screen last Wednesday evening. It brought back vivid memories from my time at public school, aged 14. There was a really unpleasant bully in my house called Peterson, who was two years above me. I once saw him urinate over the duty fag in the urinals, knowing this boy was already late for ringing the lunch bell.

At the end of the summer term, Peterson somehow managed to slip a really hard-core porn magazine into my dirty washing bag after I'd packed up my trunk and left it in the lobby. When I got home, my mother asked me to leave my dirty washing bag in the kitchen. Oh Mark, I'll never forget the look of utter horror and disappointment on my mother's face when she emptied the bag and the magazine fell open on the kitchen floor. I tried desperately to convince her it wasn't mine and that I'd never seen it before. I knew it was Peterson, but I felt powerless to say anything for fear of the repercussions that would undoubtedly follow.

I can remember Peterson knocking on my study door holding a spiked hammer and threatening to hit me extremely hard if I didn't go and bid for the rubbish in his study sale. I mentioned this to the housemaster and his only response was, 'I've never been able to take Peterson seriously.'

You said something so wonderfully healing and liberating last week after I'd mentioned those painful feelings of exclusion and being 'sent to Coventry' (I was once left to stand against the wall for nearly two hours after the master who had punished me for running in a corridor 'apparently' forgot about me). When you spoke of going from exclusion into the embrace of our loving heavenly Father, I felt the painful memories of being abused and disbelieved instantly melt away.

It reminded me of the moment in Australia when I became a Christian. I'd been invited to stay on a Christian ranch in the wilds of Eastern Victoria. The guy in charge of my wagon was called Shane – he had hair flowing way down over his shoulders and he regularly tested his faith by riding his motorbike through haystacks in The Apostles Stunt Team. He and I were poles apart on every level. I spent most of the weekend arguing with him about Christianity. As

I look back, it was amazing how Shane really loved and accepted me as a brother. He never once took the mickey out of me for my 'Prince Charles' accent and my whiter-than-white legs (I used to get called 'Light Poles' if I dared to bare my legs on the beach!).

Before leaving the ranch, we were invited to get together in a barn for a final word from Eric, the guy who had set up the ranch many years before. He was an amazing guy – a builder from Sydney, who'd had a vision to build a ranch in the Australian bush and invite young people from the cities to experience God's creation in the raw. Eric simply said he hoped that each of us had met with Jesus that weekend. As he said those words, I felt a powerful tingling sensation go from my feet to my head.

Afterwards, Eric came and found me and gave me the biggest bear-hug embrace I'd ever experienced. It sounds extraordinary, but I'd never been hugged before (my parents were not hugging sort of people).

Talk about experiencing the Father's embrace! I just broke down into uncontrollable sobs . . . and then the healing began.

FAREWELL TO THE LOCUSTS

Much of what I've written here may seem strange and even simplistic but I have found that this is the most effective way of opening up our orphan hearts to healing. When we position ourselves to enter into the healthiest attachment of all – to our Father in heaven – the positive experience of the Love of all loves displaces the negative experience of our broken attachments and gives us the capacity to declare from our hearts, not just from our heads, the positive beliefs that we need to hold about ourselves and others. When this happens, our hearts start to be restored and our brains start to be rewired. We embark on a lifestyle of choosing to think, feel and behave differently – not as boarding school orphans but as the adopted sons and daughters of God, and all this is a result of miracles more than methods.

The things we lost when we were sent away to school may never be restored to us in a literal way. We may never find our way into our father's arms, or our mother's heart. We may never return to the house that we called our home. We may never relate to our siblings with the joy that once we knew. We may never experience restoration in these areas at a literal level. But in a spiritual sense, we can experience restoration in all of these areas when we own and tell our story to people we trust. When we choose to forgive those who have hurt us and open ourselves to the Father's love, the following will become a daily reality:

1. Love
We encounter the love of our Father in heaven

2. Home
We find our heart's true home in his arms

3. Safety
We discover that the Father's love is a protective love

4. Childhood
We receive healing from childhood pain and start to dream again

5. Siblings
We experience true 'family' with our adopted brothers and sisters

6. Innocence
We have our shame transformed into honour

7. Freedom

We learn to live in the glorious liberty of the children of God

All this is restoration.

It is the only lasting answer to the awful deprivations of our boarding school years.

It is the only thing that heals the separation and the shame that stem from our experiences of abandonment.

When the time of restoration begins, the time of the locusts comes to an end.

9. THE KINTSUGI PROCESS

In November 2014, I was sitting opposite a German friend called Marius at breakfast in a hotel near Nuremburg. I was leading a writer's workshop at the time and he had asked to have a private word with me. After a few minutes it became clear that he wanted to bare his soul; he too was going through a divorce and was suffering from a broken heart and broken relationships. When we had shared our stories with each other, he asked a question.

'Have you heard of Kintsugi?'

'No, I haven't. What is it?'

'It's a form of ceramic art practiced in Japan. It dates back to the fifteenth century and it consists of taking hold of broken bits of pottery, fixing them with resin and powdering them with gold.'

'Why gold?'

'The idea is to take hold of things that are broken and regarded as worthless and then transform them into something more beautiful and valuable than they were before.'

'That's amazing. What does Kintsugi mean?'

'It means golden joinery.'

My friend paused before he concluded.

'We may be broken,' he said, 'and our relationships may be broken too, but we are in a process of golden restoration and we will be more valuable after we are reintegrated than ever we were before.'

THE DYNAMICS OF DISCONNECTION

Many people who go to boarding school end up feeling broken. This fragmentation happens in a number of different ways. The first is the silent separation between the inner, wounded, crying child and the grown-up, outwardly confident adult. The second is a split soul in which thinking and feeling become divorced, with thinking ending up dominant. The third is a gradual disconnect between a private confusion concerning who you really are and a public, often fabricated version of yourself. All of these disconnections are toxic and can last a lifetime.

These three kinds of breakage mean that many ex-boarders need the third phase in the healing process, namely reconnection. Somehow, somewhere, ex-boarders need to find someone who can subject their fractured lives to a Kintsugi process.

Take Joanna as an example, who wrote to me recently and shared her story. Watch how she describes how these different kinds of disconnection have affected her – especially the separation between yesterday's child and today's adult, and between her thoughts and feelings:

Hope Place was not your average school. A large, imposing stately home on the edge of the Derbyshire Dales, you could well have imagined you were entering the set of a Jane Austin novel. Sweeping outside steps took you up into an enormous entrance hall with marble flooring and large stone pillars. The rest of the building was no less impressive, though there was also a wild bleakness in the large draughty dormitories which were named after Scottish abbeys – where up to twelve children slept in old bunk beds and shared part of a chest of drawers between two.

To my 8-year-old self, I imagine it was very exciting to be going there, though certainly a little daunting. Being an avid reader of Enid Blyton, the school likely appealed to my very creative imagination. I am confident the adventures us girls had there could very easily have given Mallory Towers stories a run for their money!

Exciting as it may have seemed, at the end of the day I was only 8 years old and going away from home at that age is something that I imagine could be very traumatic too.

I have no conscious memories of arriving at Hope Place on that first day of the summer term in 1983. Nor do I have any conscious memories of my first term. My mum still has my first letter home, written in my first week, where I tell her Brownies meet at the school – something I do not remember ever happening there. My letter gives no indication of how I was feeling and I cannot connect (except in theory) to ever having been the bucktoothed little girl in photos from that era.

I do learn from the first letter that after being dropped off by my parents I helped my new form teacher move a table from one class to another and waited with her until my 'good neighbour' arrived to show me round. Davina was a girl in my class who was already settled at the school and had been chosen to take me under her wing until I found my feet. We soon became close friends, but I cannot get to any memories of playing or learning together. It is like someone has taken the jigsaw pieces which make up the memories of those years and wiped off the picture.

What Joanna is talking about here is fragmentation and her story indicates that this occurred at two levels.

First of all, Joanna experienced a division between her thinking and her feeling. In order to protect herself from the trauma of abandonment, she shut down her emotions. This led to her not remembering how she felt.

Secondly, she experienced a splitting into parts. Her 8-year-old part became a separate reality, a dissociated version of herself. So successful was this dissociation that she cannot identify with photos of her 8-year-old self.

Thankfully, the story doesn't end there!

Here is a poem Joanna wrote a few months ago. In it, she talks about welcoming this 8-year-old part of herself and in the process reconnecting with her feelings about her traumatic abandonment at prep school:

Who is that little girl I see, the one who's looking back at me?
The one who seems to be so sad and tries so hard to not be bad.
By nine years old you ran away, what did you really want to say?
What is the pain that makes you yell? What is it that you cannot tell?

Oh, little one, what do you feel? Was there a time when you were real?
When you so often wet the bed, what were you thinking in your head?
Who did you turn to when you cried, without a parent by your side?
How did you cope with so much muddle and painful days without a cuddle?

You also share my name of Jo, but more than that I do not know.
I do not know what you believe or how to help you when you grieve.

I cannot reach into your shame or take away the screaming pain.
I only know that you are me and Jesus came to set you free.

You're trapped inside my broken heart, a really precious work of art.
God made you beautiful and free, to clamber up upon his knee,
And trust him as your closest friend to lovingly restore and mend.
'It's over now, you're safe and well, there's nothing that you cannot tell.'

There're memories I cannot find, confined to my subconscious mind.
Instead I daily hear your pain that as of yet you will not name.
'Oh, little one, won't you confide? There's NOTHING that you have to hide.
There's NOTHING far too bad to share that can't be brought to God in prayer.'

My child, you are part of me, and I have grown up LOVED and FREE.
To keep things hidden out of sight will not expose them to the LIGHT
And give them chance to lose their power that binds me in my darkest hour.
Let's trust God's LOVE to step inside until there's nothing left to hide.

THE DISSOCIATED SELF

As an ex-boarder experiences healing, they come to embrace reconnection. Having received a revelation that they are boarding school orphans, and having started to welcome the restorative embrace of their true Father, the work of reconnecting the fractured parts of their lives can now begin. This reconnecting work can certainly be helped by psychotherapy but it is most powerfully facilitated when a person introduces their wounded, inner child to the Wonderful Counsellor. This is precisely what Joanna is doing in her poem. She is giving that 8-year-old part of her soul a voice. She is calling that child out of hiding and she is inviting her into the safest place in the universe, the arms of the Everlasting Father.

To see how this all works we need to spend a few moments unpacking the word 'dissociation'. Dissociation is the tendency we all have to dissociate from ourselves. As with so many things in life, there is a spectrum here. At the mild end, we all engage in dissociation. Have you ever been driving a car during a stressful time, looked at the road, and realized that you've just spent the last ten minutes or so in a 'zoned out' state? Have you ever been jolted back to your present reality, wondering how you've not crashed? If so, you've experienced the mild and day-to-day version of dissociation.

At the extreme end of the spectrum, however, dissociation is much more serious; it is a form of repression or denial. In the face of trauma – either sudden or accumulative – a person dissociates themselves from the self going through suffering. Looking back later, they either feel as if this happened to someone else, or they cannot remember it at all.

What we are talking about here is a defence or survival mechanism that enables us to adapt to environments that we find oppressive. At the mild end, we zone out and live somewhere else for a few minutes or hours. At the extreme end, we separate into parts. We dissociate ourselves completely from the self experiencing the trauma. If we went to prep school, that 8-year-old self, abandoned and alone, becomes stuck in a dissociated state. We only know that it is still part of us when we experience any similar scenario later on in life. Then, as the possibility of a new abandonment looms large in our minds, we find ourselves right back in the 8-year-old self, desperately afraid and deeply sad. Instead of responding out of our adult self, we now react out of the wounded, child. This either means that we overreact and leave our loved ones bewildered, or we try to create scenarios in which our loved ones are the people who now feel what that 8-year-old part of us felt.

What Joanna is talking about is dissociation – and towards the extreme, not the mild end. It is something to which many ex-boarders have resorted in order to survive the trauma of being sent away to school.

A RECONNECTION MIRACLE

We all have a tendency to shut irritating or painful realities out of our brain and we do this by going to a place in our minds where these things can no longer trouble us. In other words, we all engage in dissociation. What many boarding school pupils do is, however, very damaging. They dissociate themselves from their abandonment. In the process, that part of themselves becomes buried, sometimes for the rest of their lives.

One of the members of HALT (our Home At Last Team, dedicated to supporting those suffering from boarding school pain and those suffering from disassociation issues) is an extraordinary woman called Gill. I have known Gill for many years and she is, quite frankly, a miracle – or at least the product of one. Although Gill did not go to boarding school herself, she suffered horrendous abuse as a child. Dissociation was her defence mechanism. In other words, she dissociated herself from each of the traumas she experienced. This led to her creating multiple parts. In short, she was desperately fragmented. Having heard her tell her story, it's hard for me to imagine anyone going through a more oppressive and painful childhood.

Where is healing to be found for such fractured souls?

Gill was helped by some wonderful pastoral ministry but the breakthrough, as far as reintegration is concerned, occurred in a simple yet powerful encounter with the Wonderful Counsellor. Here is her story:

My life had hit rock bottom, I had been through several relationship break-ups and I had now hit another crisis. I had been a Christian for three years and now I had come up against something I had done at 21 years old which I was having difficulty coping with. A loving couple supported me through this crisis, but everything in my life was now shaken up.

Two months later I found my marriage in trouble. I was having very bad nightmares and went back to the couple for more support. On top of this, I now discovered that I was suffering from something called multiple personality disorder (MPD). This was over 30 years ago and very little was known about it.

I was badly abused from very early on in my childhood and my coping mechanism was to allocate each event to a different personality/person. For thirty years, I thought this was how everyone lived. Now all the small people inside of me that had been hidden were out in the open. There were many personalities all wanting to tell their story but trust had to be earned. My counsellors decided that each character needed to come to Jesus and into their Heavenly Father's arms. This was a long and traumatic process.

I received counselling for about eighteen months while I worked for a small family travel firm. This was a Catholic travel company that mainly ran pilgrimage tours. I was asked if I would travel to Medjugorje – a place in the old Yugoslavia where many years ago some children had had a vision of our Lady. The country was coming towards the end of a time of war and they wanted me to travel out to see if it was safe to take pilgrimage tours. I happily agreed, as I was weary of the counselling, what with all the pain I was constantly experiencing.

Just before I left, I read a book about a lady in the USA who was receiving secular counselling for MPD and who said she was eight years into counselling and was no closer to being whole. Before going out to Medjugorje I prayed, 'Lord, I cannot possibly go through this for another seven or more years. I need you to do something quick.'

Whilst in Medjugorje I had to climb a hill which was a tourist site. At the top of this hill were many crosses planted by pilgrims. I remember looking at the crosses and a feeling of panic coming over me. I shouted, 'No, Lord, not here! Please don't let the personalities come out here.'

But my Heavenly Father comforted me: 'You said you couldn't go through this for seven or more years so I am going to bring all the personalities together here and now. You have nowhere to run except to me.'

At that moment, my Heavenly Father poured out his love and comfort upon me in a strange land.

I came back to the UK a very different person.

It was not the end of the journey; it was the beginning of a new journey, a new way of life, a new way of living and coping.

qFor the first time in my life, I was able to be loved and to love.

THE PRINCE OF PEACE

For recovering ex-boarders, the most effective way of receiving healing and experiencing reconnection is through doing what Gill did – bringing our broken heart into the presence of the Prince of Peace.

Sometimes I think we forget what a beautiful word 'peace' is. The Hebrew word for peace – the word that the prophet Isaiah was using in Isaiah 9:6 – is *shalom*. This means so much more than what we often understand by 'peace' – the absence or cessation of conflict. Peace in the Hebraic mindset is a much more holistic reality. It refers to integration at every level of life. It denotes wholeness in our relationship with God, with others, with our inner selves, and with our environment. Peace is reconnection and reconciliation in every sphere and in the biblical worldview, this happens through Jesus Christ, who is not just our Wonderful Counsellor, he is the Prince of Shalom.

You may recall how I was encouraged by my psychotherapist to write from my adult self to my 8-year-old, prep school self. What I didn't include was how that process ended. Having finished the interaction between TM (Today's Mark) and YM (Yesterday's Mark), there was a time of silence. In that time, I began to see something. I later wrote it down:

> I saw in a vision my 8-year-old self walking in prep school uniform to Jesus, who had appeared in the form of a great lion. A huge hug

followed in which I saw my old, sobbing self wrapping his little arms around the lion's neck. As that happened, my wounded self started to disappear into the great mane of the lion. My head went first, then my shoulders and arms, my shorts, my legs, my polished black shoes – everything.

Then I saw the great lion walk to my adult self. He looked into my eyes. He smiled. Then he just looked down at my heart and said one word – 'open'. There was a door there. As soon as it swung wide, the lion hunched his shoulders and then bounded through it and disappeared. I knew he was within me . . . is within me, along with the healed 8-year-old part of me.

I felt together, whole, complete.

I felt it for the first time.

And I roared!

Truly, Jesus is the Master of Reconnection.

FALSE IDENTITY

When Joanna sent me her poem, she added this note underneath: 'I am so thankful that since writing that poem I have finally been able to connect to that broken little girl and cry out (as an adult) the agonizing pain of mother and father loss.' Please notice what Joanna is saying here. First of all, she is telling us that she reconnected with the 8-year-old part of her soul. In other words, she brought that boarding school orphan out of hiding. She led her into the light which is the presence of the Wonderful Counsellor. Urging this inner child to trust again, she created an atmosphere of healing in which reconnection could at long last happen.

Secondly, Joanna reconnected the thinking and the feeling

parts of her soul. Remember what I wrote in an early chapter about split soul syndrome. When a child is sent away to boarding school, they separate feelings from thoughts and learn to live in the mind not the heart.

When a person brings the inner boarding school orphan into the light, they not only have that part of their soul reconnected to the rest of their lives, they also find that their feelings – shut down during the trauma of abandonment – are reactivated. As Joanna puts it, we begin to give ourselves permission to give voice to the pain of father and mother loss.

There is more. When we give ourselves to this Kintsugi process, the separation between the private and the public self starts to be repaired as well. Keep in mind that one of the ways a boarder survives is by constructing a self that elicits the approval of the boarding culture. In an attempt to alleviate the secret shame caused by broken attachments, the boarder creates a version of himself based on achievement. In effect, this means finding what he or she is good at and building an identity on that – whether this is playing the fool, scoring tries, winning scholarships, whatever. This provides the affirmation, acceptance and approval that the boarder misses from their parents. The trouble is, this is an identity based on performance not position. It is conditional not unconditional. In the end, it leads to wearing a public face that may not correspond at all to the person's true identity.

How, then, is this rupture between public and private identity to be repaired?

Once again, we need to go back to attachment theory. As is now commonly recognized, those who enjoy healthy attachments with their parents have an altogether different sense of who they are from those whose attachments are ruptured:

Healthy Attachment	Broken Attachment
I am lovable	I am not worth loving
I am safe	I am unprotected
I am capable	I am powerless
I am good	I am bad
I am happy	I am sad[36]

When a child is sent away to boarding school, it is almost inevitable that they will start to believe lies about their true identity. The sense of 'I am' is distorted by the disconnection. They now begin to lack a secure concept of self; they are on the road to an unhealthy self-image.

TRUE IDENTITY

How is an ex-boarder set free from their false identity? It is here that we need to be increasingly open to the identity-shaping power of spiritual healing. When Scrooge experienced the intervention of the spirits, he eventually discovered who he really was. He was free to be. His identity was no longer the cold, controlling front that he had presented to the public. It was the warm, empowering person he once had been before his abandonment at boarding school and his discovery of the addictive power of what Dickens calls 'Gain' (with a capital 'G'). Scrooge's spiritual transformation was the key; it led him to enjoy his new, true self before it was too late.

In recent months, a remarkable story has hit the headlines in Great Britain. It concerns the Archbishop of Canterbury, Justin

Welby – an old Etonian. Many people have been very struck by the Archbishop's response to the news that his biological father was not the man Justin had thought he was, but rather a former private secretary to Winston Churchill. The nation was impressed by the humility and security displayed by the Archbishop in the face of this potentially disorientating news. Instead of reacting with the type of histrionics that typify celebrities in such circumstances, the Archbishop's reaction was measured and deeply moving.

'There is no existential crisis,' he said, 'and no resentment against anyone. My identity is founded in who I am in Christ.'

In an interview on BBC breakfast news, the *Daily Telegraph* reporter responsible for breaking the news reported on a conversation he had held with the Archbishop. When the information about the true father emerged, Charles Moore put it to the Archbishop that the reason why he responded with such quiet assurance was because he had, since becoming a Christian, found his true identity in the fact that God was his Heavenly Father. To that, the Archbishop said, yes. As his own press statement put it:

My own experience is typical of many people. To find that one's father is other than imagined is fairly frequent. To be the child of families with great difficulties in relationships, with substance abuse or other matters, is far too normal. Although there are elements of sadness, and even tragedy in my father's case, this is a story of redemption and hope from a place of tumultuous difficulty and near despair in several lives. It is a testimony to the grace and power of Christ to liberate and redeem us, grace and power which is offered to every human being.

He added, 'I know that I find who I am in Jesus Christ, not in genetics, and my identity in him never changes.'[37]

That is the voice of an ex-boarder who has found a sense of alignment between who they truly believe they are and what they present to the world.

I believe that only an ex-boarder who has entered into a healthy attachment to their true Father in heaven could say that. In this and in so many other ways, Archbishop Justin Welby is an example for many other ex-boarders, especially those who hold leadership positions.

AMAZING GRACE

Whether you are a Christian or not, it is hard not to be impressed by the transformation that happens when a person finds healing for their ruptured attachments in a healthy attachment to our Father in heaven. When this happens, a Kintsugi process begins in the ex-boarder's life. What has been disconnected becomes reconnected, even in the brain itself. The inner, wounded child is healed. The parts that we create in order to survive are reintegrated. The feeling part of the soul is reactivated, often with many and seemingly incessant tears. The private doubts about who we really are – sometimes even descending into self-hatred – are replaced by a serene certainty about our identity and a warm sense of being beloved.

What we are encountering here is *grace*, and no one has defined grace more poignantly than theologian Paul Tillich:

Grace strikes us when we are in great pain and restlessness. It strikes us when we walk through the dark valley of a meaningless and empty life. It strikes us when our disgust for our own being, our indifference, our weakness, our hostility, and our lack of direction and composure have become intolerable to us. It strikes us when, year after year, the longed-for perfection of life does not appear, when the old compulsions reign within us as they have for decades, when despair destroys all joy and courage. Sometimes at that moment a wave of light breaks into our darkness, and it is as though a voice were saying: 'You are accepted.'[38]

That is truly grace.

I wonder if you've ever experienced it.

Grace is the power that takes hold of the broken parts of our lives and carefully repairs them.

Grace is the love that reconnects the disconnected and shattered parts of our soul and tenderly reintegrates them.

Grace is the wisdom that sees how the breakages we've suffered can be used to make us of greater value to those in search of healing.

Grace does not frown on fragmentation. Grace rejoices in restoration.

Grace does not judge us for our past. Grace woos us with its futures.

Grace does not hide the damage in our lives. Grace illuminates the repairs.

We are all clay in the potter's hands – hands that are powdered with gold.

As the prophet Isaiah once declared, 'You, LORD, are our Father. We are the clay, you are the potter; we are all the work of your hand' (Isa. 64:8).

Hear the words of this loving Father – words that he spoke

to Gill as she stood upon a hill and received healing for her
fractured soul.

Make these your own:

My child, as you stand upon this hill,
Look how everything is so calm and still.
Look at the mountains all around.
Take time my child to listen to the sound
Of my voice that speaks inside of you
And listen to what I want you to do.

My child the time has come
When I want to make you one.
You may not feel ready at all
But my child I will not let you fall.
My child I want your body and soul
To come to me and be whole.

All the characters you have hidden inside,
All the characters that you have tried
To deny the right to live.
Now my child I come to give
You the freedom you so desire
Feel my love burn like a fire.

You may feel weary and weak,
You may not know how to speak,
You may feel guilt and shame,
But I gave you your name.

Every little one,
Everything they have done,
Is you.
And you knew
From the very start
How I would break your heart.
You never believed I would make you whole –
You always believed they had your soul.
Now the time is here
When you have to give me your fear.
Do not worry, do not panic, do not be afraid,
For I am the one who has paid
For the pain and torture you have been through.
And now my child it is I who want to make you new.

You will have much to talk through and share
But remember my child they will still love and care.
You will have no one to hide behind now,
But do not fear for I will show you how
To cope with the new you.
I will see you through
The trials and tribulation.
Why? Because you are my creation
And I, your Father above,
Cover you with my love.

10. ANGELS WITH BEER

The final stage of healing involves recovery from those addictions that we have used in order to mask the pain of our sense of shame. These addictions are things, people, substances, ideologies, and technologies on which we have become dependent in order to mask the ache of homesickness.

There is so much I could write here about the kinds of addiction that plague the boarded heart – sporting prowess and academic success are right up there, borne aloft as they are on the wings of a performance mindset that says, 'I need to earn love and approval through doing well.'

I could also write a lot about the kinds of substance addictions to which ex-boarders are particularly prone. Alcohol, food, drugs, etc. are all very often used and to excess during the child's exile from home, and often these are carried through into adult life.

Then, of course, there are certain behaviours that become addictive, such as the accumulation of money. The ex-boarder, like Scrooge, seeks to protect themselves through homes and possessions, exhibiting in the process the paradox of being rich and feeling poor.

There is so much I could say here about addiction, but the primary point I want to make is this: what was lost at the very moment of exile was attachment – attachment to one's father and attachment to one's mother. However defective these relationships were, this detachment was very damaging.

This loss of attachment must find some kind of compensation, some form of anaesthetic, if the child is going to survive. Inevitably, the loss of healthy attachments leads to adopting toxic attachments.

Addictions are those mood-altering agents to which we become overly attached as a means of masking and numbing the aching pain of homesickness in the boarded heart.

No one can live long in exile from the people they love most without being sorely tempted to resort to anaesthetizing attachments – such as sex and work – that momentarily slake the thirst for love.

But these things never ultimately satisfy.

When the prodigal was in the far country, he engaged in a number of addictive behaviours before he eventually hit bottom. When he did, he lost everything – except of course his father's love.

All his attempts to find what he was looking for in toxic attachments failed him miserably. It was only coming home into his father's embrace that healed him. It was re-attachment to his dad that set him free.

For every boarded heart, there is hope. In the Father's love, the trauma of desertion can be healed and deprivation can be replaced by restoration. Disengaged emotions can be reengaged;

broken relationships can even sometimes be repaired. And addictive personalities can find freedom as toxic attachments are revealed for what they are – the idolatrous attachments that are self-destructive substitutes for the healthiest attachment in the world: to our Father. When the boarded heart encounters the Father's love, the shutters are unbolted and the bright light of heaven starts to illuminate the soul, bringing with it the opportunity to live, love and laugh again, just as we did before we were sent away to boarding school.

Like Scrooge, we can wake up to a brand new life!

THE ADDICTION PROCESS

Addiction is one of the subjects by and large missing in books and articles on boarding school pain, and yet my experience of meeting up with ex-boarders of my own age is that many of us developed addictive personalities to one degree or another at boarding school. We all not only opted to intellectualize our pain ('it will be the making of us') and minimize our pain ('boarding school had its challenges but it did me no lasting harm'), we also choose to anaesthetize it and become 'comfortably numb'. This is completely understandable given the trauma of our broken attachments to our parents. Somewhere, somehow, the homesick soul has to find solace and relief. The love-hunger deep within our boarded hearts has to be satisfied. The problem, as Brené Brown has said, is that 'When we're anxious, disconnected, vulnerable, alone, and feeling helpless, the booze and food and work and endless hours online feel like comfort, but in reality they're only casting their long shadows over our lives.'[39]

If we are to be liberated from our addictions, we need to understand how we became enslaved in the first place. If addictions are essentially unhealthy attachments that we use to compensate for the loss of healthy attachments, then it stands to reason that the point of origin for addiction is **pain**. When we experience the trauma of abandonment – either as a sudden or an accumulative wound – pain, intense and enduring pain, afflicts the heart. Some children are sent away to boarding school at as young as 4, but most tend to be exiled from home around the age of 8, as I was. Others are sent away later, at 13. Whatever the age, the effect is the same – an acute and agonizing sense of being left behind and left alone, as if we were not worthy of love, not worthy of being at home.

T.S. Eliot once said that 'human kind cannot bear very much reality.' When a child is sent away to school, a hunger for the attachment they have lost now begins to grow within their homesick souls. In such a bewildering environment, the child learns that the institution cannot act as a meaningful substitute, nor can older boys and girls, housemasters and housemistresses, chaplains and matrons. Wherever a child looks, he or she soon learns that there is no substitute father or mother who can do for them what dads and mums can. The hunger for love therefore intensifies.

Sooner or later, the child finds something in their world that brings a momentary relief from the loss of attachment, affection and affirmation. This addictive agent can be any number of things: a substance (such as food or alcohol), a behaviour (academic success or sexual experimentation), an ideology (a philosophy or a belief system), a technology (such as smart phones or computer games), or a relationship (a crush or an obsessive love for another). These addictive agents allure the homesick child because they provide a temporary numbness. In short, they are mood-altering.

The trouble with these attachments is not just the fact that they cannot ultimately and permanently numb the pain, nor the fact that they prove to be toxic; it is the simple fact that they create dependency. The addictive agent or agents become, in effect, idols. They become the focus of the wounded child's thinking – thinking that becomes increasingly illogical, manifesting itself in remarks like, 'Oh, this is not doing me any harm; it's simply taking the edge off things,' or, 'Everyone's doing it.' This is in effect a cultural lie that is inevitable within an environment where many if not most boarders are living day-to-day with a secret pain that can never be acknowledged because of the danger of being called 'wet'.

So what happens? The dependency inevitably turns to powerlessness. What does addiction really mean? It comes from a Latin word that means 'to hand over'. When a person starts to develop a love for the bottle at boarding school, they hand their lives over to alcohol. For the rest of their lives one of their coping mechanisms is to drink regularly and copiously, believing the lie that they cannot get by without it. Often ex-boarders are encouraged to go on believing this deception by joining professions where an unhealthy consumption of alcohol has been normalized and even legitimized too. It will take 'hitting bottom' to wake many people out of the stupor of the effects of living in addictive social systems like these.

In all, then, the process of addiction looks like this:

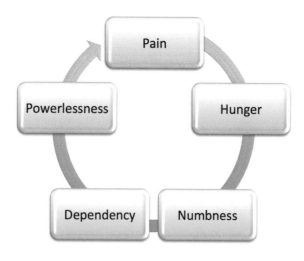

WORKING FOR APPROVAL

One of the most dangerous and insidious addictions in the boarding school culture – and one demonstrated in the lives of countless ex-boarders – is the addiction to performance. This is encouraged right from the first day. The pupil from an early age is brought quickly to the understanding that what matters most is achievement. Whether it is in the classroom or on the sports field, what matters is success – not others' success, but mine. This leads inexorably to a driven personality. Instead of working *from* approval, the child works *for* approval. Instead of growing up in a home where the parental message is, 'We love you for who you are, not for what you do,' the child grows up in an institution where the opposite message is taught: 'We will applaud and affirm you if you do well.' In a sense, this is true of most school cultures, but it is especially true of boarding schools, where astronomical fees create an even more intense drive in the child to achieve.

We must, of course, be careful here. There is a difference between being addicted to performance and striving to do one's best. The performance addiction is really an addiction not just to success but also to perfectionism – to getting everything perfect and right in the sight of others. 'Perfectionism', as Brené Brown has written, 'is the belief that if we live perfect, look perfect, and act perfect, we can minimize or avoid the pain of blame, judgment and shame.'[40] Seen in this light, we can see how intoxicating perfectionism is in a boarding school culture. When children are sent away to school, they effectively become orphans and orphans are notorious for being driven to achieve. They are fiercely competitive and jealous when others prosper. All this creates a perfectionist lifestyle designed to mask the pain of separation and shame.

This is not to say, however, that all our hard work which we dedicate to success is abnormal or addictive. Creating something that's perfect for my own benefit and simply doing your best for the sake of others are not the same. There is a world of difference between me being driven to make this book perfect, so that I will have some need for approval met, and working hard to tell my story in a way that helps other people's needs to be met. Only you and I know the difference. A fearless inventory of our motives will quickly reveal whether we are working *for* approval or *from* approval.

OUR HIGHER POWER

How is a person to be liberated from such addictive behaviours? There will be many answers to this but mine is a faith-based one. Right from the start of Alcoholics Anonymous, many have recognized that the addict needs a power greater than themselves to recover from their dependencies. That power has often been described in spiritual language, although the addict is free to choose what meaning to give to words like 'God'.

For me the higher power that brings true freedom is the Father's love. I have long held the belief that addictions are unhealthy attachments that we develop in order to compensate for the loss of healthy attachments, especially to our parents. When a person is deprived of a father or a mother, they are robbed of love. When a person is fatherless and motherless and cries themselves to sleep at night, they are sentenced to surviving not thriving. We should not then be at all surprised that boarding school orphans will start to look for love in the wrong places. Deprived of the unconditional love, honour and affirmation of their parents, they grasp for any addictive agent that gives them any resonance of the same reality, however toxic.

After over thirty years of listening to and praying for countless people, I have come to this conclusion: the only lasting, effective antidote to addiction is reattachment to the Father's love – a love that can embrace us in a mother-like way as well – as well as ongoing healing in non-judgemental, recovery families. When addicts encounter the true Father's embrace, and then commit to belonging to faith communities where broken people are welcomed and where being real is honoured, then the healing can truly begin. Yes, counselling is a vital part of the journey. Yes, group therapy is helpful. But ultimately, our love hunger will only be satisfied when we move beyond a purely psychological approach and find our way, like the prodigal son, into the Father's arms. Furthermore, our freedom will best be found and sustained in families of faith where the Father's love – our help from heaven – is encountered.

ABBA'S CHILD

Perhaps no one has written about this more powerfully than my favourite author, Brennan Manning. Ordained a Franciscan priest in 1963, he began a life of ministry to broken people outside the church. As his obituary reads:

> The early seventies found Brennan back in the U.S. as he and four other priests established an experimental community in the bustling seaport city of Bayou La Batre, Alabama. Seeking to model the primitive life of the Franciscans, the fathers settled in a house on Mississippi Bay and quietly went to work on shrimp boats, ministering to the shrimpers and their families who had drifted out of reach from the church. The fathers restored a chapel that had been destroyed by Hurricane Camille and offered a Friday night liturgy and social event there, which soon became a popular gathering and precipitated many families' return to engagement in the local church.41

Father Brennan only started writing, however, after confessing his addiction to alcohol. This led him to focus on two important themes in his bestselling and much-loved books. The first is simply the call to be real rather than religious. Perhaps my favourite quote on this is in *The Ragamuffin Gospel: Good News for the Bedraggled, Beat-Up and Burnt Out*:

> When I get honest, I admit I am a bundle of paradoxes. I believe and I doubt, I hope and get discouraged, I love and I hate, I feel

bad about feeling good, I feel guilty about not feeling guilty. I am trusting and suspicious. I am honest and I still play games. Aristotle said I am a rational animal; I say I am an angel with an incredible capacity for beer.[42]

The second theme was the importance of experiencing the love of the Father, or, to use Father Brennan's famous phrase, being 'seized by the power of a great affection'.[43] Father Brennan believed that the central revelation of Jesus Christ in the New Testament is that God is Abba. He also believed that we are created to become Abba's child. In Abba Father's arms, we are loved unconditionally. That is why Father Brennan was always keen to make sure that the people he spoke to knew that God loved them just as they were and not as they should be.

Do you believe that the God of Jesus loves you beyond worthiness and unworthiness, beyond fidelity and infidelity – that he loves you in the morning sun and in the evening rain – that he loves you when your intellect denies it, your emotions refuse it, your whole being rejects it? Do you believe that God loves without condition or reservation and loves you this moment as you are and not as you should be?[44]

ALL IS GRACE

Encountering the Father's love and being part of recovery families where being real is normal are both critical to our recovery from dependency. Thankfully, there are more and more people writing and speaking about the Father's love – more than at any time in history. If you want a story-based introduction, then I recommend you read *The Shack* by William Paul Young, one of the bestselling novels of all time.[45] Here the central character, Mac, is a man blighted by a great sadness – the murder of his daughter. One day, Mac receives a note in his letterbox inviting him to the shack where the atrocity was committed. The note is signed, 'Papa'. The invitation, it turns out, is from heaven. It is an invitation to receive healing from the great sadness and also to discover the reality of the Father's love – a love that Mac has always found difficult to embrace because his own father was an alcoholic.

What I'm talking about here – and what Young is writing about in *The Shack* – is the furthest remove from religion. I am championing two values that are largely absent in religion: relationship with Abba, Father and reality with each other. Religion promotes the idea of God's transcendence, otherness and distance. At the vertical level, it increases the sense of separation from us and God. In religious systems, including some Christian ones, God is remote not relational. Furthermore, instead of being real with one another at the horizontal level, we wear masks and play religious games, living a lie rather than lives of courageous vulnerability, transparency and honesty. In both realms, the vertical and the horizontal, religion is completely unhelpful when it comes to recovery. What we need instead is what Jesus of Nazareth came to give us – a relationship of intimate communion with our Father in heaven and lives of authenticity with each other.

This, to my mind and the minds of an increasing number of believers, is what true Christianity is. Recovery for those suffering from dependency will not come to those who participate in religious cultures where God is a distant deity rather than a doting dad, nor will it come in communities where we are kept distant from each other by rituals and regulations. It will come in communities where broken people are welcomed in a non-judgemental way, and where the Father's embrace is experienced by all as we gather to worship the God who looks like the extravagantly loving father in the story of the returning son.

Nothing else will do.

As Father Brennan Manning indicated in the title of his final book, 'all is grace'.[46]

GRACE FOR CO-DEPENDENTS

This same grace needs to be extended to all the spouses, children and other family members who are harmed by the ex-boarder's unhealed behaviour. This unhealed behaviour negatively impacts the ex-boarder's loved ones in two ways: the first is because of emotional detachment; the second, toxic attachments. These correspond to the intellectualizing and anaesthetizing components of the typical boarding school survival strategy:

INTELLECTUALIZING
- Detachment with loved ones

ANAESTHETIZING
- Attachment to addictive agents

The spouses and children of ex-boarders often become caretakers in the lives of those harmed by the boarding school system, and in that respect they become co-dependents. This co-dependency is something that turns them into people who survive rather than thrive, just like the ex-boarder. Secrecy surrounds the entire matrix of relationships because the ex-boarder shut down emotionally a long time ago. In this atmosphere of silence, shame grows.

All this goes to show how important it is for those who didn't go to boarding school, and yet who are daily impacted by those who did, to be reached by the same grace that the ex-boarder needs. In particular, those who are married to ex-boarders need support, not just while their spouse is still married to them, but after the marriage break-up if that happens.

The following story, told by a woman called Linda, shows just how the co-dependent can become damaged in the ex-boarder's world, and that they need as much support as the ex-boarder:

Steve was born in Angola, to missionary parents. He came to England aged 6 to be reunited with his sisters, who had been sent home four years earlier when they were aged 6 and 4. When his parents returned to Africa, he was sent to boarding school. He was 7, had had no previous schooling and spoke very little English, as he had been looked after by an Angolan mama and his friends were all African, so his first language was Kikongo. This of course made him a prime target for bullying. He spent most of his first year crying himself to sleep. He did not see his parents again until he was 11, when the three siblings only recognized their parents at the airport because their mother was wearing a dress the elder sister remembered from their previous furlough.

He never talked much about his boarding-school experiences, but I know they weren't happy years, and involved misbehaviour, bullying and sexual experimentation. When I first met him at the Christian Union at college at the beginning of our first year, he was like a lost soul. His clothes were in disrepair, and he had an air of sadness about him. I'm afraid my initial relationship with him was more of a mothering role, as I darned his jumpers and turned the collars around on his shirts! Our relationship deepened and eventually we became engaged during our final year at college.

Steve's home life had been with two maiden aunts, his mother's sisters, who openly admitted they didn't know what to do with boys. They took Steve's sisters on holidays and left him with his grandparents. He even acknowledged he had a hatred of women due to his upbringing.

When we left college, Steve got a teaching post and a bedsit near my home, but it soon became obvious that he wasn't coping living alone, so we brought our wedding forward to the May half-term. He suffered from bouts of severe depression and pent up anger but, in my naivety, I assumed that when he had a loving wife and a normal home life, his mental health would improve.

Sadly, his dark moods continued and put a great strain on our relationship, especially when the children arrived and I had to do my best to shield them. This meant that I always took the blame to keep the peace, if possible, but it also meant (I realize now) that Steve never had to take responsibility for his actions, nor was he encouraged to seek help for his condition, which has since been diagnosed as bipolar. He always complained that I didn't love him enough and even that I didn't know how to love. I felt that his need for love was like the proverbial black hole that can never be filled.

He constantly feared that I would leave him. During the school holidays, he would not allow me to spend time with friends as he wanted constant company, and during term time I always had to be at home when he returned from work, even though I never knew what time that would be.

Eventually, after twice seeking extra love from outside the marriage, he had a breakdown and left home to live in our caravan on a caravan site near his work, and after many months, into a council bedsit. I believe this was so that he could be the 'leaver' and not the 'left one' – although l would never have left him.

At last he sought psychological help and faced up to some of his problems, but sadly it was too late to save our marriage, and he was by then committed to another relationship – although he did admit that he would rather have been back with me, but it was too late to go back. He has since married that person and lives in Africa – the continent of his early childhood, which I'm sure is significant. His wife is very domineering and orders every moment of his life, which obviously satisfies a need inspired by his boarding school experiences, making him feel secure. He was always asking me what to do and admitted that throughout his early life he had never had to make a decision for himself – even when to change his underwear. It was all controlled by the school regime, including his career choice, which was made by his housemaster! When a family decision had to be made, he would always say, 'I don't know. You decide.'

What this testimony highlights is that all affected by boarding school pain need the healing love of the Father and the ongoing support of a recovery family (i.e. a group dedicated to honesty and liberty in the realm of addictions). It's not just the one who's been through boarding school. It's their families too. Their suffering is just as deep and lasting.

The Power of Forgiveness

In all of this, one of the most important tasks faced by all those affected by this legacy of pain is forgiveness. Here again we come to a subject that is barely mentioned in the literature about boarding school pain. This is surprising because, as I've frequently written in other books, forgiveness is the golden key that unlocks our chains and sets us free. It is forgiveness that releases us from the bitterness that acts as a levy against the floodtides of God's amazing grace. It is forgiveness that removes the boards from the boarded heart and opens up the soul to the Father's healing love.

What is forgiveness? Forgiveness is identifying those who have hurt us, naming the pain they have caused and then making the choice to give them a gift they don't deserve – our unconditional forgiveness, no strings attached. Forgiveness is one of the noblest acts a human being can ever perform. It is a sign of great strength, not weakness. When Jesus looked at his tormentors at the cross and said, 'Father forgive them,' this was not doormat ethics – it was the prayer of a man whose moral strength was unparalleled. This is something we can emulate.

If we are boarding school orphans, we can forgive our parents for sending us away from home to school. Yes, we may feel that we are being a little ungrateful, given all that they paid to get us there. But we must understand that however good the school was, and however much we may feel that this experience afforded us privileges and opportunities in life, our parents still willingly impaired their attachment to us and us to them – and that, by any other name, is abandonment.

Maybe it's time for us to forgive our parents.

Maybe it's also time to forgive the school for any damage it caused, any teachers who harmed us and any pupils who bullied us.

Even the abusers can be forgiven, although no one should underestimate the epic heroism such undeserving grace requires.

Those of you who married ex-boarders and who have suffered from their detachment and attachments – you can forgive them too.

You may not feel they have any right to be forgiven, especially if they have caused you pain, but you can still stop replaying in your head all the hurtful episodes in your past. You can stop the ones who hurt you living rent-free in the penthouse of your life.

Forgiveness is an act in which you think you're setting someone else free from the prison of your bitterness, only to find that you yourself are the one walking out of a dark jail into the sunshine of your freedom. Forgiveness is liberating for the forgiver too!

And nowhere does this apply more truly than in the arduous act of forgiving yourself.

If you sent your children away to school, you can forgive yourself.

If you have made a mess of your life because of the survivalist lessons you learned at boarding school, you can forgive yourself too, even if you feel as if you have no right to do that.

Forgiving yourself is perhaps the hardest kind of forgiveness.

When my life went off the rails, I didn't take long to forgive those who had hurt me, even though the list was long. What I found toughest, and took far longer, was forgiving myself for all the years of being emotionally detached and toxically attached. It was far harder to forgive myself for messing up what mattered most to me – my family – than it was to forgive those who had harmed me in my boarding school years. But once I forgave myself, the freedom truly began to come.

Sometimes you need to be kind to yourself and stop hating yourself. Give yourself a gift you don't deserve! Love yourself a little. At the same time, we must be clear what forgiveness does not mean.

What forgiveness does not necessarily mean is reconciliation. We have to be realistic here. Sometimes the damage is done and relationships can't be retrieved. This is simply a fact of life, and however much we believe in miracles, we also have to be wise. When trust has been eroded, it is not an easy thing to restore. While miracles may happen in relationships, this cannot be the focus. At the risk of sounding narcissistic, what is really important is for the ex-boarder to focus on their personal soul care and to move from emotional detachment to emotional intelligence. When that happens, we are submitting to the no. 1 priority, which is to change ourselves rather than change others. In embracing this transition from emotional disengagement to engagement, we begin to experience emotional health, perhaps for the first time. When that happens, relationships may end up ultimately improving, even if the parties concerned no longer live together. The reason for this is because we have at last removed the boards from our hearts and started to be real. No longer do our loved ones see the false self but the true self.

THE FATHER'S HEART

The Old Testament ends with one of the greatest promises of the Bible, about a time in the future when the hearts of the fathers will be turned towards their children, and the hearts of the children towards their fathers (Mal. 4:5–6). Notice the word 'hearts'. If this promise is going to become a reality, then ex-boarders – to name the group of people at the centre of this book – need to re-engage their emotions. The days of the boarded heart must come to an end, and those who have been boarding school orphans up until now need to receive the healing grace of the Father's love. When that happens, our hearts, as Brennan Manning says, 'are seized by the power of a great affection'. This cannot fail to impact us at the deepest, emotional level. Having lost attachment with our earthly fathers and mothers, our hearts are now impacted by the overwhelming love of the Father – a love that releases sorrow as well as laughter. After all the years of emotional repression and intellectual denial, now at last emotions are released and the real self, submerged for years, emerges.

When this happens, real relationships become a possibility. Instead of fathers and mothers relating to each other and their children out of constructed selves and with hardened hearts, now true empathy is possible – and because of that, intimacy can start to become a reality. With that, the long hard winter of frozen feelings comes to an end and a new springtime begins in which people are at last free to say what they really feel, without separation anxiety getting in the way, or the fear of people seeing who we really are.

For the hearts of the fathers and the mothers to turn, there needs to be an invasion of love from another world. Like Scrooge, we need a supernatural defibrillation. We need our cold, orphan hearts to be revived.

And so I end with an invitation to say a simple prayer.

Dear Lord Jesus,

I thank you for teaching us that God is the perfect Father.

I've been deprived of a father's love, a mother's love too, but your Word has promised that even though I may be abandoned by my father and my mother, you will hold me very close.

I confess that I'm a boarding school orphan.

Please show me my Father in heaven.

Let him walk through the mists of time and heal my wounded heart. Let him hold me in his arms.

Let him release my tears and restore the years that the locusts have eaten.

And let me find my heart's true home in the Love of all loves.

In your name, Jesus,

Amen

If you've prayed that prayer with a sincere heart, you will not be disappointed. Your Father may come to you suddenly or he may come to you gradually. However, he does and whenever he does, you will find that being attached to him is where your salvation and healing are found. All other attachments wither and die, but this attachment – to the Father's love – abides forever and satisfies the father and mother hunger in our souls.

With this kind of wholeness, we will find that our stories at last begin to move along a redemptive trajectory.

We will write the ending.

And when our lives are done, we shall have lived well and loved well. We will be able to say, in the words of C.S. Lewis, 'The term is over: the holidays have begun.'[47]

NOTES

1. Nick Duffell, *The Making of Them: The British Attitude to Children and the Boarding School System* (London: Lone Arrow Press, 2000). Joy Schaverien, *Boarding School Syndrome: The Psychological Trauma of the 'Privileged' Child* (Hove & New York: Routledge, 2015). See also Joy Schaverien's article 'Boarding school: the trauma of the "privileged" child' published in the *Journal of Analytical Psychology*, 2004, 49, 683–705 which can be accessed online at www.marcusgottlieb.com/images/articles_traumaofprivchild.pdf.

2. See Baruch Hochman and Ilja Wachs, *Dickens: The Orphan Condition* (Madison, NJ: Fairleigh Dickinson University Press, 1999). A technical and difficult read, however, and there is no chapter on *A Christmas Carol*. The authors argue that Dickens's 'ultimate loyalty is to the abandoned child' in his fiction (p.11) and that Dickens is the master of the 'orphan imagination'. 'The orphan condition entails a profound sense of having been rejected and abandoned', they write (p.14) and 'Dickens's insight into the psychology of orphanhood is profound' (p.15). It would have been interesting to have seen an in-depth discussion of Ebenezer Scrooge in light of these remarks.

3. Data's experience with the emotion chip is explored, among other places, in the 1994 movie *Star Trek: Generations* (Paramount Pictures).

4. Cited from the online version of Charles Dickens's *A Christmas Carol*, at:
www.pagebypagebooks.com/Charles_Dickens/A_Christmas_Carol/

5. Schaverien, *Boarding School Syndrome*, p.222.

6. Schaverien, *Boarding School Syndrome*, pp.222–3.
7. See Nick Duffell, *Wounded Leaders: British Elitism and the*

Entitlement Illusion (London: Lone Arrow Press, 2014).

8. Schaverien, *Boarding School Syndrome*, pp.179–191.

9. Mark Stibbe, *I Am Your Father: What Every Heart Needs to Know* (Oxford: Monarch, 2010). *My Father's Tears: The Cross and the Father's Love* (London: SPCK, 2014).

10. Brené Brown, *The Gifts of Imperfection: Let Go of Who You Think You're Supposed to Be and Embrace Who You Are* (Center City, MN: Hazelden, 2010).

11. Josy Jablons, 'An Open Letter to my Boarding School.' Available online at: http://thoughtcatalog.com/josy-jablons/2013/11/an-open-letter-to-my-boarding-school/

12. Colin Luke's TV documentary entitled *The Making of Them* was published in September 1994 (Mosaic Pictures. Copyright and video sales belong to the BBC, London). The programme is available in full online on YouTube at www.youtube.com/watch?v=2uRr77vju8U.

13. *Goodbye Mr Chips*, a novel about a boarding school teacher called Mister Chippings, by James Hilton (London: Hodder & Stoughton: 1934). The most memorable film version is with Robert Donat, 1939 (MGM, directed by Sam Wood). Some of the scenes were filmed at Repton School.

14. Nick Duffell, 'Surviving the Privilege of Boarding School' an online PDF: www.boardingconcern.org.uk/downloadlibrary/SurvivingthePrivilege.pdf.
15. I am quoting from the version cited in *USA Today*, 8 December 2015:www.usatoday.com/story/life/entertainthis/2015/12/08/benedict-cumberbatch-wrote-loveliest-letter-santa-claus/76973876/.

16. Duffell, 'Surviving the Privilege of Boarding School' online PDF.

17. Duffell, 'Surviving the Privilege of Boarding School' online PDF.

18. Joy Schaverien, *Boarding School Syndrome*, pp.179–91.

19. Peter Clothier, *The Making of Them* TV documentary review, 28 September 2014. www.huffingtonpost.com/peter-clothier/the-making-of-them-tv-doc_b_5896504.html.

20. Clothier, *The Making of Them review*.

21. Jeremy Clarkson's comments, published in an article in *The Independent*: www.independent.co.uk/news/people/jeremy-clarkson-opens-up-about-bullying-at-public-school-i-was-made-to-lick-the-lavatories-clean-and-10336723.html. His comments originally occurred in a Sunday Times column in which he was reviewing the new Range Rover.

22. John Thorn, *John Thorn's Road to Winchester* (London: Weidenfeld & Nicolson, 1989), p.153. Thorn, headmaster during my years at Winchester College (1974–9) described the spirituality of the college chapel as 'non-infectious semi-religion' and of the vastly different character of the revival of Christianity that occurred during his time as headmaster.

23. *Lady in the Water*, written and directed by M. Night Shyamalan (Warner Bros, 2006). This film was scathingly reviewed by Mark Kermode in one of his famous rants. See www.youtube.com/watch?v=z8HVurzYdUw.

24. Mark Stibbe, *John as Storyteller: Narrative Criticism and the Fourth Gospel* (Cambridge: Cambridge University Press, 1994).

25. Brené Brown, *I Thought it was Just Me (but it isn't): Making the Journey from 'What Will People Think?' to 'Am I Enough?'* (New York: Avery, 2008).

26. *Galloping Foxley*, a short story by Roald Dahl, is available in full online at http://users.cybernet.be/philippe.burniat/6e1/galloping%20foxley.pdf. The *Tales of the Unexpected* TV adaptation is available in full on YouTube at https://www.youtube.com/watch?v=8FyzRNgkmV8.

27. Dan Goleman popularized the term 'emotional intelligence' in his 1995 book with the same title, although it was first used in 1964 by Michael Beldoch.

28. Stibbe, *I Am Your Father*, pp.159–61 and pp.170–72.

29. Juvenal, *Satire* X (356).

30. Nick Duffell and Thurstine Basset, *Trauma, Abandonment and Privilege: A guide to therapeutic work with boarding school survivors* (Abingdon & New York: Routledge, 2016), p.5.

31. Mark Stibbe, *I Am Your Father*, p.130–77.

32. See Jeremy Holmes, *John Bowlby and Attachment Theory* (Hove & New York: Routledge, 2nd edn, 2014).

33. *The Railway Children*, 1970, directed by Lionel Jeffries, starring Jenny Agutter as Bobbie.

34. Edith Nesbit, *The Railway Children*, (1906) http://www.learnlibrary.com/railway-children/railway-children_chapter_xiv__the_end.htm.

35. Ted Dekker, *A.D. 33* (Nashville, TN: Center Street, 2016). All quotes are from his introduction, 'My Journey into A.D. 33'.

36. I am indebted to Colby Pearce, *A Short Introduction to Attachment and Attachment Disorder* (London & Philadelphia, PA: Jessica Kingsley, 2009), p.36.